BUILD IT

AND THE MONEY WILL COME

Master the 5 Secrets to a successful
Building & Property Development business

Tony Dimitriadis CPA

'I have personally known Tony for about twelve years and have also been a client of his during this time. His responsiveness, dedication and professionalism are next to none. His personality is very warm, intelligent and genuine. Tony is very focused on providing you with the best advice for your circumstances. I would definitely recommend Tony as an adviser (and friend) to any potential business or individual.'

– Sally Schmidt, Loyalty Director at Xero

'Tony and his team at AD Partners have looked after all our personal and business accounting needs and our insurance needs since day one. Tony has remained professional, accessible and trustworthy throughout our twenty years of dealings and I have no hesitation in recommending Tony to anybody who needs an accountant of the same qualities that Tony and his team at AD Partners portray day in day out. Thanks for your ongoing support and commitment to us and all our financial needs, Tony. We look forward to many more years working together.'

– Aysun Portoglou, Business Development Manager at Aussie

'I have had the pleasure of working with Tony now for over ten years and he is, without a doubt, one of the most professional and hard-working consultants I have had the pleasure of working with, both as an accountant and as a client of his, but also as a professional that I have engaged for complex work both in Australia and offshore. I can highly recommend Tony as a professional consultant, and also as an accountant to all; he is someone who definitely embodies the right work ethic and the right qualities as an individual, which are a rare find and combination. Thank you for many years of great and consistent work.'

– Damian Cessario, DLC Capital

'Tony at AD Partners has shared his experience, expertise and advice, which have been invaluable in allowing me to make sound decisions both on a personal and professional level.'

– Anna Mastwyk, Learning and Development Consultant

'I have been a client of Tony's for many years now and have been very happy with the level of service and attention to detail that he and AD Partners have provided. Now also as a client of AD Wealth I look forward to continuing that excellent relationship.'
  – Aldo D'Alberto, Business Manager at Polymers International Australia Pty Ltd

'I have been a client of AD Partners since commencement of their business. Tony has always been very professional, well informed, diligent and very intelligent – nothing is ever too much trouble or bother. I can rely on Tony to help me with everything that needs his expertise; he always seems to have the answer to everything that needs to be sorted out. I feel sure and confident that I will continue to receive his exceptional service and great advice as I continue to require and need it.'
  – Rose Tibaldi, Retail Consultant Gandel Group

'Thank you for the outstanding service you provide with both my professional and personal requirements. You are always on hand to answer my questions, and your staff and management are great to deal with. I have always felt that I am treated like a person, not a number. Thank you, Tony – I have already recommended you to friends and colleagues. After ten years the service hasn't changed.'
  – Rosanna Cittadini, Director – Service Tech Australia

'I have been a client of AD Partners for over 15 years. They have a professional team experienced in all fields of taxation and financial planning. They oversee my investment portfolio to always assist me to achieve the best possible returns.'
  – Anthony Craus, Property Developer

'I have been dealing with Tony and the team for over five years now and am delighted to have them as my accountants and financial planners. They are professional and always there to give credible advice when required. I could not recommend AD Partners more highly.'
  – Kel Kilner, National Sales & Marketing Manager at True Foods

'As a long-time client of AD Partners, I recommend them to anyone and everyone. Prompt, professional and perfect! The 3Ps.'
  – Andrew Martin, Director – Room 35

First published in 2017 by Grammar Factory Pty Ltd.

National Library of Australia Cataloguing-in-Publication entry:
Creator: Dimitriadis, Tony, author.
Title: Build it and the money will come : master the 5 secrets to a successful building and property development business / Tony Dimitriadis.
ISBN: 9780995445314 (paperback)
ISBN: 978-0-9954453-2-1 (eBook)
Subjects: Business enterprises--Finance.
            Real estate development--Finance.
            Real estate business.
            Success in business.

Printed in Australia by McPhersons Printing Pty Ltd
Book production by Grammar Factory
Editorial services by Grammar Factory
Cover design by Designerbility
Typeset in 10.5/15 pt Acumin Pro by Independent Ink

Disclaimer

The material in this publication is of the nature of general comment only, and does not represent professional advice. It is not intended to provide specific guidance for particular circumstances and it should not be relied on as the basis for any decision to take action or not take action on any matter which it covers. Readers should obtain professional advice where appropriate, before making any such decision. To the maximum extent permitted by law, the author and publisher disclaim all responsibility and liability to any person, arising directly or indirectly from any person taking or not taking action based on the information in this publication.

I would like to dedicate this book to all the ambitious business owners working tirelessly in the building and property development industry.

I hope that the ideas and tips in the book help you to build and live your dream.

CONTENTS

INTRODUCTION 1

Build it and the money will come... 4

Who am I? 5

Keep it simple, stupid... 8

CHAPTER 1: STRATEGY **9**

Where are you going?... 11

Defining your mission statement 11

Creating a vision statement.. 16

Defining your values 18

Setting your one- to three-year goals........................... 22

Where are you now?... 26

Profit and loss statement... 27

Balance sheet.. 30

Statement of cash flow.. 34

Putting it all together... 36

How will you get there?.. 38

Business benchmarks.. 38

Key performance indictors... 42

Taking action 44

Measuring your progress... 46

Summary.. 46

CHAPTER 2: STRUCTURE **47**

What are the options? 48

What should you be thinking about? 52

    Asset protection 52

    Tax minimisation 57

    Control 60

    Active or passive income 62

    Cost 63

    Ease of administration 65

    Ability to adapt 66

    Succession planning 67

Summary 69

CHAPTER 3: STATUTORY **71**

Compliance requirements 73

    Tax 73

    Superannuation 74

    Workers' compensation 75

    Payroll tax 77

    Land tax 78

    Stamp duty 81

Summary 84

CHAPTER 4: SYSTEMS **85**

Managing cash flow 86

    Creating a cash flow forecast 87

Maximising your working capital 90

    Managing payments to suppliers 91

    Managing work in progress 93

    Managing debtors 95

Managing finance 97

    Getting the most out of debt finance 99

    Refinancing 105

Troubleshooting 106

Summary 108

CHAPTER 5: SUPPORT **109**

Working with a virtual CFO versus doing it yourself 113

What are the different ways a virtual CFO can help
you and your business? 115

How do you choose a virtual CFO? 116

CONCLUSION **121**

APPENDICES **125**

Appendix A: Taxation issues for property developments 127

    Tax on mere realisation of a capital asset 128

    Tax on profit-making transactions 130

    Tax on income-generating businesses 131

    When your property development changes 133

    Summary 136

Appendix B: Structuring your property development 137

    Special purpose vehicles 138

    Joint venture arrangements 140

    Development agreements 144

    Self-managed super funds 145

    Summary 153

Appendix C: Property development and GST 155

    An introduction to GST 155

    Do you need to register for GST? 156

    How do business losses affect GST? 159

    What concessions are there for GST? 160

    Can you avoid the GST pitfalls? 166

    When should you consider cancelling your
    GST registration? 171

    Summary 173

Appendix D: The Small Business Restructure Rollover 175

    Uses for the new rollover 176

    Consequences of rollover 178

    The loss denial rule 181

    Interaction with Small Business CGT Concessions 182

    Case study 183

    Summary 185

ACKNOWLEDGEMENTS 187

ABOUT THE AUTHOR 189

ABOUT AD PARTNERS 191

INTRODUCTION

'The secret of getting ahead is getting started.'
– Mark Twain

You are an ambitious business owner who wants to make a mark on the world.

You want to achieve your personal goals, whatever they may be.

In business, you want to achieve financial stability and take control over your business and your life.

You want to live a lifestyle that enables you to have more money in your pocket and more time to use it, in any way you choose.

But how do you do it?

Business is tougher than ever in today's competitive world with more than 60 per cent of small businesses failing within the first three years, and 75 per cent failing within five years, according to the Australian Bureau of Statistics.

As a result, you need to be as strong as the concrete slab you lay when building. Just like when you're constructing a building, your business needs to have a strong foundation. You need to have the right people working for you and with you to build your business and your lifestyle.

You face many challenges in your business and they all have an impact on your ability to earn the *money* to give you the *lifestyle* you want.

But this is easier said than done. How can you retain your rightful share of the money you earn? How can you effectively manage the cash flow requirements of your business so you can access money when required for development or investment? How can you access financial information in real-time to make informed business decisions? And how do you get your head around the difference between cash and profit; tax, GST, CGT; and ensure your business generates a return on your investment?

You need to understand and accept these challenges. You need to embrace them and face them head on. You can't afford to bury your head in the sand. You also can't afford to take shortcuts, and you can't afford *not* to get the right people in to help.

Meeting these challenges is the key to the financial management of your business.

Money can be a beautiful thing and at the same time it can be a nightmare. With it, you can do so much. Without it, you feel helpless.

You need money in your building and property development business to invest in land and property. To acquire equipment and machinery. To pay for labour and resources. You also need to fund the project through to completion. Then, at the end of the project, you would definitely like to have some left over – the more, the better.

Without money, the project, no matter how big or small, will suffer. In the worst-case scenario, it won't even get off the ground.

Your money needs to be managed correctly, right from the beginning. If your business is not structured right so it suits your particular situation, then you are destined to lose money from day one. The wrong structure will mean that, even after all your hard work building and developing, you will give up to half of your profits to the government. I don't think you want that to happen. Do you?

Worse still, without the right structure and foundation for your business, all your personal assets will be at risk should something go wrong. Many unforeseen circumstances arise and you could be exposed and potentially lose it all.

Like money, with people, you can do so much. Without them, you can feel overwhelmed, trying to do everything yourself.

People are great, but only when you have the right ones around you to provide support. This isn't the case when you don't. With them, you can achieve so much. Without them, you run out of power or battery, just like your favourite trusty drill.

When you are working on a job in your building or development business, I am sure that you get the right specialists for the parts of the job that are outside of your specific expertise. Even if you have the expertise, you want to have someone else do that particular part so you can concentrate on something else.

Well, it should be no different when it comes to the financial management of your business. If you do not have the expertise, then you need to get it yourself or someone who does.

Ask yourself: do you truly understand financial reporting? Do you understand the difference between cash and profit? Do you understand the difference between income and capital? Do you understand your return on investment? Do you understand tax law and compliance? Are you planning and budgeting? Are you managing your cash flow?

The reality is you need a high level of financial intelligence to be able to be successful in business today, and likely even more so in the future.

You need to find the right people for the job. If I want to build a house or develop a block of land, I will go and find the right person to help. Someone just like you. If you want to optimise your business's finances, you'll need to do the same.

BUILD IT AND THE MONEY WILL COME

In this book I will teach you how you can better financially manage your business so that you have more money in your pocket to fund the lifestyle you want.

You can achieve this by following five simple steps, each outlined in the book's chapters:

1. **Strategy:** The first step in any journey is deciding where you want to go. In the first step of my framework, you'll create a strategic plan by assessing where you are now, deciding where you want to go, and charting the most efficient course between the two.

2. **Structure:** The right structure can save time, money and heart-ache. The wrong structure, on the other hand, can make your business far more expensive and complicated than it needs to be. Structure is an essential piece of achieving your strategic goals, so in this step I'll outline what you need to consider when it comes to choosing the right structure for you.

3. **Statutory:** Are you aware (and on top of) all of the obligations you have to the Australian Taxation Office (ATO), Australian Securities and Investment Commission (ASIC), State Revenue Office (SRO), Land Titles Office, WorkCover Authority, your superannuation provider and your bank? This is a major stumbling block where businesses in building and property development can unwittingly

subject themselves to fines and liability. In Chapter 3, I'll cover the main obligations you need to be aware of as an ambitious business owner.

4. **Systems:** If you are trying to manage everything by yourself on an ad hoc basis, not only is this inefficient, but you run the risk of not meeting your statutory obligations. In this step I'll share the main money management systems your business will need to stay on top of your obligations, while moving towards your strategic goals.

5. **Support:** As an ambitious business owner, you probably try to do it all. After all, it's your business – you want to make sure everything's running as it should be. The problem is that this isn't sustainable – you can't be all things to all people, and you can't do everything at the high standards you'd like. This is why support is essential. In Chapter 5 I'll teach you how to find the right support team to help you implement the first four steps of the framework, while pushing your business on to bigger and better things.

In these five steps, you will find all the tools you need to grow a financially rewarding, tax-efficient, lifestyle business.

WHO AM I?

My name is Tony. I am a Certified Practising Accountant (CPA) and have successfully run my accounting practice, AD Partners, for over 15 years. We are based in Melbourne; however, we have worked with many businesses across Australia.

As an ambitious business owner myself, I very clearly understand the challenges you face as I have experienced some of them myself. I know how it feels when payroll's due, but you're still waiting for a big payment to come in. I've had the difficult conversations with staff members about not delivering work on time, or to the standards we need. And I get what it's like to feel like you're on your own, and like you have to do it all yourself. The pressure you put yourself under by thinking that way is enormous. It doesn't have to be that way. In fact, it most definitely should not be that way. By putting in place the right systems, you can relieve yourself of all that pressure because the right systems will deliver the right results. I will give you the tools to achieve this later in the book.

I hold the financial qualifications and experience having worked with over a thousand business owners across a wide range of industries, including building and construction, property development, hospitality, retail, manufacturing, automotive, IT, health, finance and transport, just to name a few. While there are differences between those industries, there are also many similarities that the business owners within those industries experience.

I have helped structure and restructure over 500 hundred businesses, laying the strongest foundation to help them build and grow. One client, for instance, was operating his business as a sole trader, which meant he was paying *49 per cent* of his profits in tax. By restructuring his business to a private company, we were able to cut his tax to 27.5 per cent, saving him over $50,000 in the first year alone! Unsurprisingly, his tax savings have improved his cash flow and allowed him to reinvest in his business to grow even further.

I have also helped establish future planning initiatives for many of my clients to create long-term wealth. Another client was accumulating his savings and earning 2.5 per cent in interest in a term deposit, yet paying 40 per cent of that interest in tax. While he liked his money to be secure and readily accessible, it wasn't achieving the growth he ultimately wanted. Instead, I established a self-managed superannuation fund for him which is earning him a 7.5 per cent return, on which he only pays 15 per cent in tax. Just imagine how much faster his wealth is growing now!

I have saved business owners from near bankruptcy, completely turning their financial positions around. Most recently, a client in severe financial distress was contemplating closing the doors and walking away. Imagine if you will, a bright, intelligent woman, who had been in business for 10 years. Like most entrepreneurs, she had a wonderful family, who she loved and cared for – 2 daughters and a hard-working husband. As we all know in this room, running a business is not easy. For 'Beth', it was a dream that was quickly becoming a nightmare. As most entrepreneurs know, we sometimes live on the edge of our businesses – Beth was no different, except that her business was about to collapse and take down with it, the lifestyle that she had truly enjoyed with her family up until that point...it really wasn't looking good – the books were a mess – her business was in freefall...and she was staring bankruptcy up close and personal.

I took it upon myself to find out what was really happening, and brought the end to a new beginning. It became very clear to me that she was suffering from the same 3 major problems that all businesses suffer in her position – lack of financial intel, the wrong structure and no systems.

We sat down and I showed her how to do what needed to be done. We started by putting in place a strategy on how we were going to get back on track. We established the right structure for the business. We then mapped out all the statutory obligations and put in place the systems required to make it efficient and seamless. Finally, engaging the right support team to keep her moving forward.

Today, she has a profitable, cash-positive, debt-free business and is grateful for her second chance and really making her mark.

In the industry, I am best known for offering my clients a complete financial solution and helping them achieve their financial goals much sooner and with significantly less concern and frustration along the journey.

After working with me, my clients feel extremely assured and positive about the future. They are taking back control of their business, delivering remarkable value and creating amazing opportunities to truly benefit their business and ultimately their lifestyle.

This book will help you achieve that lifestyle.

KEEP IT SIMPLE, STUPID

It can be easy to overcomplicate things, especially when it comes to the financial and regulatory aspects of business.

I find that, in most circumstances, the KISS (Keep It Simple, Stupid) philosophy is the best strategy. Consequently, *Build it and the money will come* aims to keep things simple, so you can get a bird's eye view of your business to figure out what's working, what isn't and how you can improve to achieve even greater levels of success.

While more complex thinking and strategy may be required at times, the more I can simplify matters for you, the better you'll understand and the better placed you will be to move forward and grow.

CHAPTER 1: STRATEGY

'If you fail to plan, you are planning to fail.'
— Benjamin Franklin

Every time I jump in my car to drive to a new destination, I have two options.

The first is to start driving and hope for the best. Unsurprisingly, that rarely ends well.

The second is to make a plan.

The good thing is I can use the navigation system in my car to help.

In my navigation system, I first program my desired destination, or where I want to go. Using GPS, the system then figures out my starting point, or where I am now. Once it has these two points, it will calculate the best route and it will tell me how to get to my destination.

Travelling through the journey of business is similar to driving a car. You must first determine your destination. You must first ask yourself, 'What do I really want?' or 'Where do I really want to go?'

You do this by creating a strategic plan.

A strategic plan will allow you to be in a position to control outcomes. Why? Because you have a clear direction and focus. This control will allow you to manage change and put the necessary steps in place to achieve what you want done. Why? Because it's an on-going process, not something you do once and then just forget about. You do not print it out and stick on a shelf in your office and think it's all done. A strategic plan will provide you with better awareness of what's needed and therefore the opportunity to influence the future. Why? Because you are living it every day. All your business decisions should be based upon your strategic plan. If they aren't, your likely to veer off track and end up somewhere else (that is, not where you wanted to be).

A good idea is just that – an idea. A strategic plan can turn that idea into reality. It's the 'how to' in the process, while the idea is the 'what'. The strategic plan gives you clarity in not only the 'what', but also the 'how'. It's when the business gets real and actually starts to do things that you want and that's what makes a difference.

You may get lucky from time to time and an opportunity may fall in your lap (seemingly, from nowhere). That is fantastic. But is it sustainable? No, it's not and I'm sure you know that.

Your client's needs will likely change from time to time and the market generally will also change. By being in tune with your clients and the market overall, you will already know these trends. It may even keep you a step ahead because you'll be in a better position than your clients because you have the industry knowledge and therefore the power to influence, in order to achieve a positive result.

You will lose valuable momentum and lead time if you are reactive rather than proactive. The strategic plan helps you establish what needs to be done and when, so you can take the right actions when necessary, rather than waiting for opportunities to come to you (or running around fighting fires as they flare up). This will then increase your momentum, enabling you to tick off all the steps in your plan even more efficiently. Ultimately, you'll be able to achieve your goals faster.

So how do you create a strategic plan? Just as when you're plotting your path to a new destination, your strategic plan should cover:

- Where are you going?

- Where are you now?

- How will you get to your destination?

The foundation of your ideal strategic plan will confirm your purpose, your goals and your objectives (where am I going?). It will ensure you understand the current state of play (where am I now?). It will encourage you to analyse the current environment and finally, it will set the right path to success (how will I get there?).

WHERE ARE YOU GOING?

The first step in creating a strategic plan is to decide where you want to go.

Unfortunately, most people never take the time and effort to determine what they want. Consequently, most people lose their way. They don't know if they're on the right road to success. Instead, they are stuck in the heavy traffic of life without any destination in mind.

So how can you be different?

Following are a number of exercises to help you get clear on your business destination, so make sure you have a pen and a paper ready.

Defining your mission statement

The first step in choosing your destination is defining your mission statement.

A business mission statement defines your goals, ethics, culture and behaviour. A complete mission statement defines what the business does, not only for its owners, but also for customers, employees and the community as a whole.

A personal mission statement, on the other hand, is what you want to focus on, accomplish and become in your personal life. It is what guides your actions, behaviours and decisions towards what is most important to you.

As the owner of your business, the two will most likely be closely aligned.

Some examples of mission statements within the building industry include:

- **Bunnings:** Our ambition is to provide our customers with the widest range of home improvement products at the lowest prices every day, backed with the best service. Our team members are the heart and soul of our business.

- **Lend lease:** To create the best places. We work closely with clients, investors and communities in Australia, Asia, Europe and the Americas to create unique places. Places that leave a positive legacy and inspire and enrich the lives of people around the world. We do this through putting safety first and delivering innovative and efficient solutions which provide long term sustainable outcomes for a range of stakeholders.

- **Metricon:** We're all about building homes where you'll truly love to live.

The benefits of having a mission statement which defines who you are, what you do and the values that guide you are:

- Marketing your business to potential clients – differentiating yourself from your competition by specialising in a certain field or product or target client. Becoming the best at what you do.

- Assist you in your business planning – as it sets the scene as to why you do what you do. It can help your business attract finance, investment and/or business partners.

- Gives you purpose and motivation – far beyond just making a profit. It will help guide you to determine the types of products and services you will provide.

- Helps you with your decision-making – providing you the framework within which you will operate. It's your compass, your map, your steering wheel.

- Provides direction to help you through the challenges that business will throw your way – by keeping you focused on what you want to achieve. Sometimes, the easy decision will create a short-term fix. Your mission will help you make the long-term beneficial decision to ultimately get to where you want to go.

If you don't have a mission statement, on the other hand, you will find yourself having to spend time and resources rectifying poor communication and unwanted cultural behaviour whether that be with clients, employees or other stakeholders. Communication is extremely important in business and it is incumbent upon the owners of the business to clearly communicate to internal (employees and contractors) and external (clients, suppliers, banks and so on) parties their desires for their business. If all parties do not know what the owner wants to achieve, the business will likely not get there, despite the owner's efforts. Poor communication will lead to poor decisions and ultimately, poor results – whether that is labour-centric (processes) or material-centric (supplies/suppliers). Both can have significant adverse effects if not managed well and the key to that is communication.

So how do you define your mission? Start by answering the following questions:

- Why did you decide to go into business for yourself? What were the drivers which led you to make that decision? Was it centred around your own personal desires or that of family, or did friends influence you?

- Who is your ideal customer? Who do you want to provide your services to? Is it private clients or other businesses? Is it residential or commercial? How will your service make a difference in their lives?

- What do you want your business to be known for? How do you want your customers and the general public to view your business? How will you influence that view?

- What are the essential products and services you will provide? How will they be different to your competitors? How will you position yourself in the market? Will it be based on price (low-end) or quality (high-end) or a mix of both?

- How will your level of service differ from that of your competitors? What will you do differently? How will you be better? Do you know their strengths and weaknesses? How will you take advantage of that?

- What type of business owner will you be? Will you lead by example? Will you delegate responsibility and authority? Will you empower your employees? Will you mentor your employees?

- How will you interact with your suppliers? What type of relationship will you have with them? Will you want to have a close relationship with few or a distant relationship with many? How can they help? How can you help them?

- Will you use technology to your advantage? How will this work? How will it benefit you? Will your processes be more efficient?

Answering the above questions will confirm to you why you are in business and what it is exactly that you really do.

Once you have an idea of why you do what you do and what your business stands for, it's time to put it into a single statement – a mission statement.

A mission statement will require your time and effort, however, it will be well worth it.

After working through the questions above, I recommend you speak with all the people connected to your business, not matter how big or small your business is. You will gain some great insight into what it is you do well and, if the conversations are honest, some things you might need to work on. They are just as important to you in your business. You should take advantage of the things you do well and work hard to improve on those things that you do not do so well, because they are important to the success of your business. That is where you will derive the most benefit and see an upward spike in your business.

Take the time to do this thoroughly and completely. While a mission statement is generally rather short (that is, only up to a few sentences), it is important for you get the right words together to truly define your mission. Use words wisely to best describe your mission. Less is more, but only if it tells your story.

Once your mission statement is complete, it should be a part of all your marketing and advertising. It should be what drives your business and excites your customers.

Creating a vision statement

A vision statement is a clear and concise long-term goal. It should be both challenging and inspiring and therefore motivating for all stakeholders.

One take on the vision is the BHAG, or Big, Hairy, Audacious Goal, coined by Jim Collins in his bestselling book *Built to Last*. He explains that, 'All companies have goals, but there is a difference between merely having a goal and being committed to a huge, daunting challenge – like a big mountain to climb ... a true BHAG is clear and compelling and serves as unifying focal point of effort.'

As I mentioned before, a vision is inspiring and challenging, which drives all stakeholders to reach the goal. Having said that, the vision has a clear finish line and, as such, can be measured and potentially achieved.

Consider the following vision statements:

- **Microsoft:** A computer on every desktop and in every home.

- **Google:** To provide access to the world's information in one click.

- **Toys R Us:** Our vision is to put joy in kids' hearts and a smile on parent's faces.

- **WWF:** We seek to save a planet, a world of life. Reconciling the needs of human beings and the needs of others that share the Earth.

- **John F. Kennedy:** Landing a man on the Moon and returning him safely to Earth (before the decade is out).

- **Wikipedia:** Imagine a world in which every single person is given free access to the sum of all human knowledge.

What all of these visions have in common is that they are *big*. They cannot be achieved in one year, five years or even ten years, in most cases. They are *hairy*, as the person or organisation that created each of those visions had no idea how they would achieve the challenge. And they are audacious, having never been achieved before.

A vision gives you something tangible to aspire to. It is bold and exciting and provides you the motivation to achieve something exceptional and something you truly believe can happen, albeit beyond your current capabilities.

For this reason, your vision statement should be outside your comfort zone. Something that will require genuine effort while giving you the motivation and inspiration along the journey. Written well, your vision statement will guide you and keep you focused. It should be so compelling that everyone involved is truly inspired.

Here are the key issues to consider when creating your vision:

- Think long term – ten-plus years into the future.

- Think BIG – the ultimate you could possibly achieve.

- Make it sharp – crystal clear and concise.

- Show your true passion – what burns inside you.

- Tell everyone that matters – employees, customers, family and friends.

- Be committed to the cause – it will take time, effort and resources to achieve.

As best you can, you need to condense all this into a single statement, as this statement can then be used to inspire you, your customers, your suppliers and the general public.

Defining your values

Values are the guiding principles that dictate your behaviour and actions. In both your personal and professional life, your values can help you determine whether or not you're on the right road to reaching your goals. They are your GPS.

Your values influence the choices you make, in both your personal life and how you conduct your business.

Examples of some personal values are: the fundamental importance of family, maintaining a healthy work/life balance and that all people should be treated equally.

Examples of some business values are: being environmentally friendly, giving back to the community, or a commitment to innovation, such as Apple based on its motto, 'Think Different.'

Why should you have values?

Some of the key benefits include:

- They help you find your purpose in life and what's important to you. If you don't know what's important to you, how can you know what you want from your life? When you answer this question, it will become so much clearer for you.

- They help you clear out the clutter. Whether in business or in life, we are consumed by so much around us. You get caught up in things that you may really not want or need or even believe in. Your values will help get rid of all that unwanted baggage.

- They help you make the right decisions, both personally and professionally. Your values will keep you focused if you are true to them. People makes decisions based on emotion far too often and therefore stray from their core values. Be clear on your values. Be clear on what you want. Always make the right decision.

- They help guide you to act in accordance with what's important to you. You will naturally do and say the things that matter most to you. Your core values are who you are and when tuned into them, you will act accordingly.

- They help you to react in difficult situations. Like decision-making, when we are faced with a difficult scenario, we can act on impulse or with emotion, therefore not thinking about our response. Before reacting, stop, think and consider your values and what's important to you. Your answer may well be very different.

- They help you to gain compatibility with all personal and business relationships. You will be drawn to people of similar values as you will rate them highly and similarly, and others will be drawn to you. You will work better with people aligned to your values and your relationships will also be stronger on a personal level.

- They help to increase your overall confidence. When you know what's important to you, then other people's opinions and thoughts do not matter. Your values will give you stability and therefore confidence to do what you want to do.

- They help with your overall happiness. You will have a purpose, clear out the clutter, make right decisions, react well in difficult situations, improve relationships and become increasingly more confident. How can that not help with your overall happiness?

The problem is that many people and businesses say they have certain values but, when push comes to shove, their actions are incongruent with the values they claim to uphold. For example, a builder who says he prides himself on his work, but who cuts corners to make a higher profit, values money more than he values his workmanship. Similarly, a builder who purports to value high customer service standards, but leaves a job half-completed to attend to another from a customer who gives him multiple jobs, also values money more than he values true customer service.

S. G. Night said is best, 'The truth is in your actions.'

Unfortunately, there are many of us that struggle with this concept, whether that is because of the fear of missing out, greed, or simply wanting to please everyone and putting their values ahead of yours.

So how can you determine your true values, rather than just listing a range of attributes you'd *like* to have?

Dr John Demartini, a human behavioural specialist, educator and best-selling author, explains that values arise from our voids, in other words by what we perceive as most missing. What you perceive as most missing (void) in your life therefore becomes what you perceive as most impor-tant (value). The bigger the void, the more important the value. The more important a value is, the more discipline and order you will have associ-ated with it.

To determine what these are, Demartini has developed the Demartini Value Determination Process – a 13 question assessment centred around what you do, how you do it and how you think and feel about it.

Demartini's 13 questions are:

1. Look carefully and specifically at how you fill your personal or professional space. What are the three items that you fill your space with most? What three items stand out in your space?

2. Look carefully and accurately at how you spend your time. What are the three things that you spend your time on most? You will make time for things that are really important to you and you will run out of time for things that aren't.

3. Next, look at how you spend your energy and what energises you the most. What are the three things that you always find energy for? You will always have energy for things that are truly highest on your values list and that inspire you.

4. How do you spend your money and your resources? What are the three things that you spend your money on most? You will feel reluctant to spend money on things you perceive to be unimportant.

5. Where are you the most ordered and organised? Where do you have the highest degree of order and organisation? What are the three things that you are most organised in? Where are you most organised?

6. Where are you most reliable, disciplined and focused? What are the three things you are most reliable on? Whatever is highest you value, you will be disciplined to do.

7. What do you inwardly think about most? What are your innermost dominant thoughts? What are the three things that you dominate your thoughts on?

8. What do you visualise most about how you would love your life to be that is gradually showing fruits and coming into reality? What are the three things that you visualise, envision, or daydream about most and bringing about?

9. What do you internally dialogue with yourself about most that is meaningful and that is gradually coming true or into your life?

What are the three things that you internally talk to yourself about most that are manifesting?

10. What do you most talk about in social settings? What are the three things that you converse with others about? What are the three things that you keep wanting to bring into conversations?

11. What inspires you or are you inspired about most? What is common to the people who have inspired you? What is common to all the things, insights, experiences or events that have repeatedly inspired you?

12. You are most willing to stretch yourself and persistently act towards goals that have the most meaning to you. So, what are the three most consistent long-term goals that you have persisted working towards that have stood the test of time?

13. What topics of study inspire you the most? When you enter a bookstore, which section do you make a beeline for? Which topic of magazines do you subscribe to? Which section of the newspapers do you turn to first? Are there nonfiction TV shows or film documentaries that you seek out?

Setting your one- to three-year goals

Having established your mission, your vision and your values, you now need to put in place the steps to get there. Your need to narrow down your focus to shorter term thinking and start listing the goals you need to meet in the next one to three years. These will become the milestones you need to hit in order to achieve your vision.

For example, if your vision is to have a $10 million business, you'd start with looking to achieve your first million, then doubling it, then hitting $5 million, and then hitting your ultimate goal of $10 million. You need to start planning how you can achieve your first milestone of $1 million. That could involve steps such as: marketing and advertising in your target markets; part-nering with other builders or property developers; establishing referrals arrangements with real estate agents; hiring the specific tradespersons you need; engaging the right contractors.

Establishing these goals has the following additional benefits:

- They help you streamline your decision-making and allow you to be more productive. Breaking down the milestones will help sharpen your focus to concentrate on smaller tasks which are more readily achievable as you move forward.

- They help you to effectively resource your business knowing exactly who and what you need. It is far easier to resource smaller tasks as you go. It will enable you to be very specific and use only the specific resources required for each individual step in the process.

- Hitting your short-term goals is a sign that you are moving towards your longer-term goals. If you are not hitting them, you have time to make any necessary adjustments to keep moving in the right direction.

- Experiencing smaller wins along the way gives you more confidence in your business and your abilities, and this keeps you motivated to reach your big vision. Achieving these goals also allows you to experience a sense of achievement and satisfaction along the way, rather than having to wait until you achieve your big vision because that will take time.

If you do not take the time to set these short-term goals, you will struggle to achieve any results (and may not even notice when you do). However, the real danger is that you may never achieve your long-term vision.

How can you set effective goals? You need to be SMART.

The SMART goal-setting method is one way to help you set more effective goals, which then makes you more likely to achieve your ultimate goals. You do this by setting goals that are:

- **Specific:** What do you specifically want to achieve? Do you want higher revenue, to hire more staff, to work with more clients, to increase your profits? Or do you want to be able to take more time off and live a better lifestyle because of your business?

- **Measurable:** How will you measure that you have been successful? When it comes to revenue, what number do you want to hit? How many people do you want to hire and how many clients do you want to work with? How much time would you like to take off? How much income do you want to be earning?

- **Assignable:** Who is responsible for achieving this goal? Is it you or someone else? Will it be a team effort and, if so, who's responsible for what?

- **Realistic:** Is the goal realistic? Is it achievable, given your available resources? Or will something need to change (the goal, the timeframe or your resources) to make it realistic?

- **Time-bound:** When do you want to achieve your goal? Do you have any other business or personal activities that may impact your timeframes?

Let's say you want to expand your business from Victoria to New South Wales. While that's a good starting point for a goal, you would need far more detail to make it a SMART goal.

Instead, consider the following: 'I will open my building premise and commence operations in the heart of Western Sydney, NSW, on 1 February, with a building manager and contractors specialising in each of the main trades – carpentry, electrical, plumbing, bricklaying, roofing, plastering, tiling and painting.'

See the difference?

Now that you have that goal qualified as your major milestone, the next step is to break it down further into mini-milestones, as follows:

- Hire a full-time building manager for the New South Wales operation, with eight to ten–years of experience and a Diploma of Building and Construction qualification.

- Find a suitable business premise of 1,000sqm in the western suburbs of Sydney.

- Attain all relevant New South Wales licences and insurances.

- Hire the required number of relevant staff – a casual administration clerk, a commission-based sales representative.

- Set up agreements with subcontractors in each of main trades – carpentry, electrical, plumbing, bricklaying, roofing, plastering, tiling and painting.

- Update website and all social marketing with new branch contact details and set up promotions for the new Sydney operation.

- Advertise in all local newspapers in the greater Western Sydney area.

- Contact all real estate agents in the greater Western Sydney area seeking referral agreements to property developers and other builders.

These should all have specific timeframes according to their priority to ensure you meet the 1 February deadline. You need to determine which mini-milestone may be dependent on others and what would work best for your particular operation. You should also assign each of those milestones to someone, whether that is you, an existing manager or an independent specialist, such as a recruitment company or real estate agent. They key is to get things done. Or, as the Dent organisation would say, #GSD – Get S#%T Done.

WHERE ARE YOU NOW?

Now you have set your destination – both your big vision and the one- to three-year milestones you want to hit in order to achieve it.

The next step is to determine whether you're on the right road to reach it.

How do you figure out whether you're on the right road? You need to review your daily routine and activities. You need to assess your income and savings. On a personal level, you'll need to consider whether your discipline and attitude will take you to greater heights in the future. And you need to review whether your knowledge and skills are sufficient to bring better results.

In other words, you need to know where you are now. It's only when you get a realistic idea of your current position that you can chart a course from where you are now to where you want to be.

This will involve reviewing your financial statements. Financial statements provide information on how your business is operating financially and why it's achieving its current levels of performance. They tell you what you've already done and whether you're already travelling in the right direction (don't worry if you aren't – there are plenty of opportunities to improve). They will also give you insight about what you need to do next. They will enable you to focus on the aspects of performance that are the most critical for your current and future success.

So what do you need to look at? The key statements are your profit and loss statement, your balance sheet and your statement of cash flow.

Profit and loss statement

The profit and loss statement is a summary of your business income and expenses over a period of time. You or your bookkeeper or accountant can choose the period you want to review in your accounting software, but profit and loss statements are also formally prepared annually for compliance purposes.

Your profit and loss statement will show the income your business has generated and the expenses incurred in generating that income. The end result is a profit or loss for the period. In other words, the profit and loss statement shows you whether your business is making (or losing) money.

Revenue, or sales, is generally quite straightforward, although if your business has different types of revenue, you can list them all separately so you can monitor how much of each of them you are generating.

When it comes to expenses, there are many different kinds. The largest expenses in the building and construction industry are generally materials and labour. Labour can be further broken down into subcontractors and wages. In addition, there are labour on-costs, such as superannuation, WorkCover and payroll tax, depending on the size of your workforce. Then there are further operating expenses such as motor vehicles, equipment hire, tools and supplies. Following on from that you have administrative expenses, such as accounting fees, bank fees, registrations, subscriptions, insurance and more. If you operate from a business premises, you will also have occupancy expenses such as rent, gas, electricity and water.

SAMPLE PROFIT AND LOSS STATEMENT

SALES

Residential Construction	1,274,982
Other Income	87,047
	1,362,029
GROSS PROFIT FROM TRADING	**1,362,029**

EXPENSES

Accountancy	4,886
Bank Charges	2,941
Cleaning	814
Depreciation	8,391
Donations	250
Electricity & Gas	3,471
Filing Fees	292
Freight & Cartage	600
HP & Lease Charges	27,018
Insurance	21,585
Interest Expense	2,562
License Fee	645
Materials	65,598
Motor Vehicle Expenses	3,689
Office Expenses	2,030
Rates	3,126
Subcontractors	668,230
Subscriptions	218
Superannuation	38,456
Telephone	2,827
Tipping Fees	1,467
Supplies	252,908
Water	1,457
Tools & Misc.	2,908
Work Experience	272
Wages	141,643
WorkCover Expenses	3,315
	1,261,599
Profit before income tax	**100,430**

The sample profit and loss statement shows two types of income streams, Residential Construction and Other Income. You are free to break this down as much as you want, remembering that you should make it relevant and something that you wish to see and track.

For example, the Residential Construction income could be broken down further into jobs that you may perform on contract for a larger home builder and jobs you source privately. Another option may be to break it down by the type of jobs, such as new builds, renovations and so on. It will involve a little more work to classify the different types of income, however, it could prove useful when it comes to analysing which parts of your business are most profitable.

Expenses are generally classified as per their type and there aren't generally major variations here. You will see on the sample profit and loss statement that the major expense types are materials, supplies, subcontractors and wages. These will be your largest expense types, as your building operation requires both types of resources in every job. Of course, there will be some smaller jobs that may have a greater labour component as a percentage of the total cost, but the same could be said about materials.

It is very important that you track your major expenses very closely as that is where you can either make some money by generating a good margin, or lose money by overspending in materials and supplies and/or not having an efficient labour force. In the sample profit and loss statement, the total percentage combined of these two expense types is over 90 per cent. On the surface, that appears to be very high; however, it may be acceptable if you had a very large job in that financial year and had to forego some margin to win the job as, generally, the larger the job, the smaller the margin percentage. Conversely, the smaller the job, the higher the margin.

It is important to continually monitor these percentages to ensure that they meet your targets. If you quoted a job and the margin you built in to that job was 25 per cent, then you need to make sure that your total costs on that job did not exceed 75 per cent. If they did, then something has gone wrong.

By managing your income and expenses well, you should hopefully see a good profit on the bottom line. What is a good profit, you might ask? That will depend on the size of your business. However, at a minimum you will want to generate a profit of approximately ten per cent after you have paid yourself a wage that is equivalent to fair market value for your services. In other words, what you would get paid if you were doing the same job for someone else.

Preparing your profit and loss statement on a monthly and yearly basis will help you track your progress towards your goals. You should review it as regularly as you require, and with the benefit of technology and cloud accounting systems, this could be live on a daily basis on your electronic device while you're on a job site. So there is no excuse not to know where you are with your financials at any given point in time.

Balance sheet

The balance sheet gives you a picture of your business's financial health at any given point in time. It lists in detail the various assets your business owns, the liabilities your business owes and the value of your equity (or the net worth of the business).

The assets of your business can include cash, debtors, stock, land, build-ings, equipment, machinery, vehicles, furniture and so on. The liabilities of your business, on the other hand, can include trade creditors (suppliers), bank overdraft, loans, tax, superannuation and so on.

The net value of your assets and liabilities is your equity in the business. It represents your accumulated earnings or losses as at the date of the report from the commencement of the business/company. Equity is also money you put into your business, whether that is once-off at start up or on an ongoing basis, although, technically it is likely to be categorised as a loan.

SAMPLE BALANCE SHEET

SHARE CAPITAL AND RESERVES

Retained earnings	2,278
TOTAL SHARE CAPITAL AND RESERVES	2,278

Represented by:
ASSETS
CURRENT ASSETS

Cash at Bank	22,681
Petty Cash	2,448
Debtors	15,423
GST Paid	151,765
TOTAL CURRENT ASSETS	192,317

NON CURRENT ASSETS
Fixed Assets

Plant & Equipment – at Cost	22,091
Less Provision for Depreciation	(4,164)
	17,927
Motor Vehicles – at Cost	121,298
Less Provision for Depreciation	(72,552)
	48,746
Furniture & Fittings – at Cost	1,367
Less Provision for Depreciation	(1,367)
	-
Total Fixed Assets	66,673

Intangible Assets

Formation Expenses at Cost	1,691
Less Written Off	(1,691)
Borrowing Costs Sinking Fund	842
	842
TOTAL NON CURRENT ASSETS	67,515
TOTAL ASSETS	259,832

LIABILITIES
CURRENT LIABILITIES

Customer Deposits	20,385
Trade Creditors	8,422
GST Collected	164,877
HP Loans < 12 Months	10,511
HP Interests < 12 Months	(1,681)
ATO Integrated Account	(5,208)
Superannuation Payable	13,456
PAYG Withholding Payable	25,636
TOTAL CURRENT LIABILITIES	**236,398**

NON CURRENT LIABILITIES

HP Loans > 12 Months	25,353
HP Interests > 12 Months	(4,022)
Admin Charges	(175)
TOTAL NON CURRENT LIABILITIES	**21,156**
TOTAL LIABILITIES	**257,554**
NET ASSETS (LIABILITIES)	**2,278**

On your balance sheet, assets are divided into current and non-current assets. Current assets are those that can be more readily turned into cash on a shorter-term basis, such as debtors and stock. Non-current assets, on the other hand, are those assets that you use to help you generate income on an on-going basis, such as plant and equipment, motor vehicles and so on.

By listing your assets in this way, your balance sheet tells you about the liquidity of your business, or how quickly and/or easily you are able to pay your bills as they fall due. This is based on how quickly you can turn your assets into cash. Cash gives you some protection when business may be a little slow and also gives you more options for growth when you are wanting to expand your business.

Every business requires assets to operate, and these assets will be funded from equity, profit and/or from borrowing money from others, typically your bank. A healthy position for your business is one where the assets are funded by profits rather than being heavily reliant on you or your bank, as I discuss in Chapter 4. However, there will be occasions where you require funding from a bank or some other source as you upgrade plant and equipment or motor vehicles, even if your cash position is a healthy one. Utilising this funding source will then leave some cash in the business for your day-to-day operations so you are meeting all of your other commitments without any concern.

While current assets can be turned into cash quickly, non-current assets are those that you use for longer-term benefits, such as motor vehicles and plant and equipment. They depreciate in value during their life, which can be claimed on your tax return.

Liabilities are obligations the business needs to pay. Current liabilities, such as trade creditors (suppliers) are generally funded by cash, hence the importance of monitoring your cash position and ensuring you have the required cash on hand to meet all your short-term commitments. Your non-current liabilities are those that have a longer obligation, such as bank loans.

You ideally want to have a manageable level of debt and, if you are reducing your debt, that is a positive sign for your business. If, however, your debt levels are high relative to your cash flow and you are required to pay interest and/or principal of your loans, this is a warning sign for your business.

You can see that there are various financial indictors in your balance sheet, just like your profit and loss statement, so reviewing this on a regular basis is very important. In fact, it should be done as regularly as your profit and loss, and depending on your cash or debt position, possibly more so.

Statement of cash flow

A common question people ask is, 'Where did all my money go?' Sometimes it's a throwaway line or said in jest but, more often than not, it is a very serious question. Unfortunately, the reason people ask this question is because they do not fundamentally understand how cash flow works. They do not have control over their money. Instead, it controls them.

Cash flow is not measured at a point in time as it continues to flow, just like the energy runs through your building or the water through your pipes. It is constantly changing with funds flowing in and out of your business.

However, you can review your historical cash flow, which is often a good indicator of future patterns if you don't change anything. You can review this in your statement of cash flow.

It is important report to understand where your money has been spent and for what purpose. Your business may have significant revenues and therefore it is easy to think that it is profitable, but should you have an issue with the collection of those revenues it will have a significant impact on your ability to meet your financial obligations. Your inability to meet payments to suppliers, contractors, employees and other creditors will stifle your ability to grow (or worse, to be able to continue to operate). Should you reach this point, you would be insolvent and potentially out of business. Not a good place to be.

Your statement of cash flow gives you a clear picture of your cash flow by allowing you to look back in time (I recommend starting with the previous three to six months) to see when your money is coming in, how much is coming in and where it's coming from. These cash inflows include revenues from selling your products or services, interest and dividends, rent, sale of business assets, loan receipts and any other business-related receipts.

Your statement of cash flow will also help you understand where you are spending your money, or cash outflows. These include payments to suppliers, contractors and employees; overhead costs, such as rent, utilities, insurance and so on; taxes, such as GST, PAYG withholding and PAYG instalments; capital equipment purchases; and loans given and repayment of existing loans.

SAMPLE CASH FLOW STATEMENT

CASH FLOWS FROM OPERATING ACTIVITIES

Receipts from customers	1,355,863
Payments to suppliers and employees	(1,264,853)
Finance costs	(29,580)
Net cash provided by operating activities	**61,430**

CASH FLOWS FROM INVESTING ACTIVITIES

Proceeds from sale of property, plant and equipment	(4,600)
Proceeds from sale of intangibles	(305)
Other liabilities received	5,044
Payments for property, plant and equipment	1,091
Net cash provided by investing activities	**1,230**

Net increase in cash held	62,660
Cash at beginning of financial year	(39,979)
Cash at end of financial year	22,681

You should be as detailed as possible as the more detailed you can be, the less chance there is of you overlooking something. You can then look forward to project what is coming up for the next period.

Of course, you will also need to consider any known seasonal or one-off factors. For example, periods of time where you shut down for holidays, when you will not be receiving money but will likely have some commitments to pay, such as annual leave for employees, rent on your business premises and all associated outgoings mentioned earlier. It is very rare in the building and property development game to have a constant flow of income and expenses on a consistent basis. You know very well that large transactions happen at various points throughout the year and the bigger the project you're on, the bigger the transactions. This is all the more reason to get this right.

Putting it all together

After reviewing your profit and loss statement, balance sheet and statement of cash flow, it's important to put all of that information together to give yourself a holistic view of where your business is now.

One effective exercise to assess this is a SWOT analysis. If you haven't come across this before, SWOT stands for Strengths, Weaknesses, Opportunities and Threats. The exercise requires you to reflect on your business's internal strengths and weaknesses, as well as external opportunities you can take advantage of, and threats you need to protect yourself against.

Strengths	Weaknesses
· What do you do well? · What do you do better than others? · What unique resources and/or processes do you have? · What do others in your industry see as your strengths? · What factors get you a sale?	· What could you improve? · What should you avoid? · What does your business lack? · What do others in your industry see as your weaknesses? · What factors lose you a sale?
Opportunities	Threats
· What opportunities can you see in your industry? · What interesting trends do you see? · What can you do that others are not? · How can you turn your strengths into opportunities?	· What obstacles do you face? · What are your competitors doing? · Is regulation threatening you and/or your business? · Is technology threatening you and/or your business? · What threats do your weaknesses expose you to? · Do you have cash flow problems?

Once you have completed your SWOT analysis, you will have brought to the front of your mind some really important issues for your business, some good and some not so good. The truth is, they are all good to get out in the open so you can do something about them.

So, what do you do?

For each of the quadrants, you need to consider how you can use that information to your benefit:

- What opportunities can you take advantage of? How can you use your strengths to take advantage of these opportunities?

- Which of the threats can you address today, using your existing strengths?

- How can you minimise your weaknesses? Are there opportunities you can leverage to do this?

- How can you avoid or insure against the threats you listed?

For example, if you have identified one of your business weaknesses as lack of labour and equipment and have identified a major growth development in your area as an opportunity, then a strategy for you may be to strengthen your resources to be able to successfully quote, win and undertake the large development project in your area.

Knowing your strengths is great, taking advantage of them is something else. Knowing your weaknesses is also great, doing something about them is really something else. This analysis shows you how, and gives you the first steps to move closer to your big vision.

HOW WILL YOU GET THERE?

Now that you understand your current position, it's time to map out how you will get from where you are now to where you want to be.

The rest of this book will be sharing strategies you can use to streamline your business to help you achieve your goals and, ultimately, your vision. For now, though, a good starting point is determining benchmarks for your business and setting key performance indicators to lower your costs, improve your efficiencies and increase your profits.

Business benchmarks

The use of business benchmarks can help you can gauge where your business is in comparison to other like businesses. This isn't about trying to be the same; it's about trying to be better.

For example, if you find that your business is spending far more on labour as a percentage of your sales than most other businesses like yours, you need to ask yourself why. Is your business more labour intensive because of the type of jobs you do? Do you pay too much for your labour? Do you employ too much labour? Do you utilise your labour efficiently? Do you have a low cost of materials? Is your labour/material mix combined more or less than the industry average? While there could be genuine reasons for your specific labour percentage, it is critical you know not only what it is, but *why* it is.

Reflecting on where your business stands across a range of common benchmarks can give you tremendous insights into what needs to change, and how you can achieve your goal. In some cases, a small tweak might be enough to save thousands of dollars a year, and in others a major change might be required. The most important thing is that, once you look at the numbers, you'll know what's wrong and you'll be able to make an educated decision about your next steps.

Which benchmarks should you be focusing on? The common ones include profitability and expense management and return on investment.

Expense management

In the building industry, the main profitability measure is benchmarked on net margin, rather than gross margin, so it takes into account total expenses before tax.

As there are a number of different trades within the building industry, benchmarking against your specific trade is important. If you are spending 90 per cent of your turnover on expenses (therefore making a ten per cent profit), but businesses in your trade typically only spend 75 per cent on their expenses (therefore making a 25 per cent profit), that's a sign that there are areas where you could improve. On the other hand, if you're making 25 per cent profit in a trade that averages 15 per cent profit, that is a sign that you're doing something right.

Here are some examples of the different business benchmarks for a few categories in the building industry (across Australia) based on turnover of greater than $500,000:

Trade	Carpentry	Tiling	Electrical	Plumbing	Painting
Total expenses	80–90%	75–85%	75–85%	80–90%	75–85%
Materials	30–40%	20–30%	30–40%	30–40%	20–30%
Labour	25–45%	25–45%	25–35%	25–35%	35–50%

As you can see, there is a ten to 15 per cent variation on each measure, as each individual business will have its own operational setup and processes. Irrespective of which trade you operate in, the philosophy is the same – you need to know where you fit and whether you are achieving the best returns you can for your business.

Note that the above figures are only a guide and not a definitive target you should work toward. Your main focus should be what you can improve to create a greater margin and, hence, a greater profit.

Return on investment

Another key benchmark is your return on investment (ROI). This tells you whether or not all the effort put into the business is returning an appropriate level on the equity you have invested.

Most financial experts will tell you that your ROI is the most important measure of all, a statement that I endorse. Why? The answer is simple – your ROI shows whether your business is worth all the effort you put into it.

You want to ensure you are getting a good return on all of the time and money you have invested in your business. If not, you may as well be working for someone else on a wage and save yourself the trouble.

Now, of course, as an ambitious business owner I know you don't even want to consider that, but it's important you get rewarded for your blood, sweat and tears.

So what is a good return?

Unfortunately, I cannot give you the exact dollar figure or even percentage because the reality is, your business is different from that of your competitor down the road. What I can give you, though, is a way to work out if you're achieving a good return. You simply need to work out whether your operating profit is greater than the cost of capital.

How do you do that?

The DuPont Analysis.

The DuPont analysis is a performance measurement that was created back in the 1920s and has stood the test of time as a simple but powerful way to determine the financial performance of your business.

It is the way for you to convert your profit and loss statement and balance sheet into a meaningful analysis of your ROI by demonstrating the return you are generating on your assets and equity. You can then determine what drives that return, and whether you are earning the return you want.

For a free copy of my DuPont Analysis template, go to www.adpartners.com.au/dupont.

It is very simple to use. You just need to enter the following information:

- Gross revenue

- Variable expenses

- Fixed expenses

- Interest expense

- Other income

- Total assets

- Total liabilities.

The excel worksheet will then calculate your various ratios and confirm your ROI.

Once you perform the analysis on your current numbers, you can then change some numbers around to see what the impact would be if you were to make some amendments to your business. For instance:

- What if you increased revenue by two per cent while keeping costs at the same level?

- What if you reduced expenses by five per cent while maintaining revenue at the same level?

- What if you reduced interest expense by three per cent?

- What if you reduced or increased assets by five per cent?

You will see the impact these changes have on your profit margin, your asset turnover and ultimately your return on assets. Now you're starting to really see where your business is financially and what you need to do to get you to where you want to be.

Key performance indictors

The next area to consider is your key performance indicators (KPIs). While benchmarks are external measures that help you determine how your business is performing in comparison to other businesses, KPIs are internal measures you can use to improve your business. Think of them like a system of levers – if you pull and push them in the right way, they can lead to higher turnover, lower expenses and more profit.

How does it work? First, you'll need to list the common elements in your business that contribute to turnover, expenses and profit. Some examples are:

- Cost of materials (as a percentage of turnover)

- Cost of labour (as a percentage of turnover)

- Hourly/daily cost of labour (dollar amount)

- Average project rate (dollar amount)

- Average project margin (as a percentage)

- Cost of finance (as a percentage of turnover)

- Return on net assets

- Debtors days

- Cost of rectification

- Actual vs. quoted costing (dollar amount)

- Actual vs. quoted time (in days or hours)

- Days lost

- Customer satisfaction

After you make a list of areas to measure, review your profit and loss statements from the past six months to figure out average figures for those areas. What is your average cost of materials? What is your average cost of labour? Write it all down.

Once you have your historical numbers, you can use these to set new KPIs. Ultimately, you want your profit and turnover to go up, so you might set a KPI for the average amount you charge for a project to increase by five per cent. At the same time, you want your expenses to go down, so you might set a KPI for your cost of materials that is two per cent lower than the percentage you currently spend on materials.

While the focus of this book is your business's financial health, you can set KPIs in every part of your business. There could be KPIs for the number of sales calls that need to be made each week, or the number of quotes you produce and possibly more importantly, the percentage of quotes you convert to sales. You could even have KPIs for your debtor collection process! Whichever ones you choose should be based on what is important in your particular business and the key areas that drive your business.

So write down your new KPIs – these will then act as a scorecard for your progress towards your goal.

If your KPIs are moving in the direction you want, that's fantastic! If they aren't, then it's time to consider whether you're taking the action you need to make them happen, or if they are realistic KPIs in the first place.

Taking action

Your benchmarks and KPIs act as short-term goals for you to hit in order to meet your longer-term goals and big vision. However, they won't help you achieve that vision unless you take action.

For this reason, it's important to develop a list of immediate action steps you and your team can take to hit your KPIs and benchmarks.

Examples of some immediate action steps include:

- Review the cost of materials from your suppliers. Are you buying the right materials at the right price from the right suppliers? You may be buying timber from the same supplier you buy your tools from for convenience, but you may be able to get the same quality timber from another supplier for a cheaper price, or better quality timer at the same price.

- Review the cost of your labour – both employees and contractors. Are you utilising your employees well? Do they get allocated first? Do they get allocated to the right jobs? How do you use your contractors? Are there minimum rates you need to pay? Are you using them on the right jobs?

- Set up clear payment terms for your customers. Do they know when to pay you? Are there progress payments? Is there an upfront payment?

- Negotiate payment terms with your suppliers and then stick to them. Can you convert cash-on-delivery suppliers to account? Can you extend 14-day accounts to 30 days?

- Follow up all quotes issued within seven days or, if you know that they are looking to make a decision sooner, make sure you contact them before that date. Do you set reminder calls for issued quotes? Do you contact them to offer advice or suggestions on how their project could be improved or managed better?

Once you have developed your action list, you can then rank your actions in terms of importance, based on the impact they will have on your business. Those that are the highest priority should be the ones that are costing the most time and money as well as causing the most pain to you, your team and your customers. Meanwhile, those that are minor inconveniences can wait until after you've addressed the big issues.

You should also ask yourself which of the action items can be completed quickly and easily, because they will be the items that give you the quickest wins and improve your position immediately. That will then give you the breathing space you need to start tackling those areas that will take a little more time to rectify.

It is all about working smarter, not harder, to start to improve your position. That is not to say that hard work won't be involved, but it just makes sense to tick off the tasks that require less effort at the beginning.

MEASURING YOUR PROGRESS

It's important to keep in mind that this isn't a 'set and forget' process. Instead, you'll need to measure your progress regularly to ensure that you are moving towards your goals. Or, to continue our driving analogy, you need to keep checking the GPS to make sure you're driving in the right direction.

Once you establish your plan, you must measure it against how you are actually performing. If you do that, it will drive you to act. To get things done. #GSD.

By checking your profit and loss statement on a monthly basis, for example, you can see whether the average margin on your jobs is increasing, decreasing or staying the same. Benchmarking your margins and comparing them to your KPIs can then highlight whether there is more room to improve, or if you're meeting (if not exceeding) your expectations. This will greatly help you not only manage your business and minimise any financial problems, but it will help you see whether you are moving closer to, or farther away from, your goals.

If you effectively measure your performance, you will achieve superior results.

SUMMARY

Your strategic plan is the roadmap that will set you on the path to success. By having a clear understanding of where you are now, and where you want to go, you can chart a course between the two and create the life-style business you deserve.

CHAPTER 2: STRUCTURE

'I thrive in structure. I drown in chaos.'
– Anna Kendrick

Building and property development relies heavily on laying a strong foundation.

As you know, the foundation is the most important part of the entire structure. It holds it all together. The ground on which we all stand is not as sound and solid as most of us think, so a properly built foundation is essential for supporting buildings over the shifting land beneath them.

If the foundation is weak, it will fail. When it does, cracks will appear internally and externally. Windows and doors will become misaligned. Floors will become uneven, slope and even crack. These problems multiply as you go up to the next floor and so on. The result? Disaster.

While the foundation itself will differ depending on whether you are building a single storey property or a multi-level development, *every job* needs the strongest foundation for its particular purpose.

It is no different when it comes to your business – you need the right foundation for your needs. Whether you are in carpentry, electrical or plumbing;

residential, commercial or industrial properties; a sole business owner or in a partnership and more. The same principle applies: you need the right structure.

The benefits of having the right structure are that it saves you money by reducing the amount of tax you need to pay; it gives you flexibility when it comes to distributing profits and adding or removing partners; it enables you to grow without any adverse effects; and it gives you peace of mind, knowing that you are set up not only for today, but for well into the future.

If you don't have the right structure, on the other hand, it could cost you your business.

Ideally, you want to get your business structure right from the beginning.

To do this, first you need to understand what your options are. Second, you need to know about the key considerations that you should keep in mind when choosing the right structure for you.

WHAT ARE THE OPTIONS?

Depending on your particular situation, the choice of structure could be narrowed down considerably as some options will not be appropriate for your needs.

The basic structures are as follows:

- **Individuals.** This is when you run your business as a sole trader, holding your ABN in your own name. This is the simplest ownership structure and is how most businesses get started. If your business generates an income, that is recorded as part of your personal income for taxation purposes, and the same goes if your business generates a loss. This structure would suit the smaller business where it is essentially just you and the net profit you generate is less than $80,000 per annum.

- **Partnerships.** A partnership is when two or more parties join forces to establish a business. A partnership is a formal agreement and requires its own ABN, tax file number and tax return. However, it doesn't pay tax, as any income it generates is divided between the partners and recorded as a part of their personal income. Similarly, any loss the partnership incurs is also divided between the partners and recorded against their respective individual income tax returns.

- **Companies.** A company is a structure that is usually used for businesses, with one of the main benefits of this structure being the tax on profits. The general company tax rate is 30 per cent, however, the company tax rate for small businesses (businesses with aggregated turnover of less than $2 million) is only 28.5 per cent. *Please note: the government has announced a reduction in the small business tax rate from 28.5 per cent to 27.5 per cent for the 2016–17 income year. The turnover threshold to qualify for the lower rate will start at $10 million. Legislation is pending.* For this reason, it is a popular choice for businesses with high levels of income, as they would otherwise be taxed based on the owner's individual income tax bracket (which is often much higher). It also provides flexibility in the number of owners, otherwise known as shareholders.

- **Trusts.** A trust is similar to a partnership or a company, in that it's a separate structure (meaning, legal entity) used to own assets and/or operate a business, so requires its own tax file number and tax return. Any income generated is distributed to beneficiaries, which is then recorded as part of their personal income. While there are different types of trusts, the most popular is the discretionary trust, otherwise referred to as a family trust. This particular trust has added tax benefits, as you have the discretion to distribute the net income any way you wish and therefore can choose to give more income to beneficiaries who are on the lower tax rates. In addition, the incorporation of a company trustee will provide personal asset protection.

- **Superannuation funds.** The final option is running your business through a self-managed superannuation fund (SMSF). An SMSF is not prohibited from running a business, however, there are many activities that are prohibited or limited when operating under this structure. As a result, you would need to carefully consider whether this structure is a suitable option for you and your business. Many of the mainstream business types in building and construction are not suitable for this type of structure. However, a property development business that is operated for the sole purpose of providing retirement benefits for the members might be suitable. Even still, due to the significant legal restrictions, I would strongly recommend seeking specialist advice if considering operating such a business within a self-managed superannuation fund.

Any of the above structures could potentially suit your particular situation – the key is finding the right one for you. Each structure is going to depend on your particular circumstances and, as a result, should be tailored accordingly with all relevant factors having been considered.

Let me run through a recent client example. A business owner based in the south-eastern suburbs of Melbourne was operating his business as a sole trader. While this structure was suitable for the first few years, his business then grew quite rapidly after winning some large contracts.

He came to see me for advice on what he should do moving forward. After establishing that this influx of work was not a one-off scenario, and his intention was to continue on this basis in the medium to long term, we discussed his tax concerns, as the projected income levels would move him into the highest income tax bracket. That would mean he would lose almost half his profit in tax, a potential situation he was not at all happy about.

He also raised concerns about his personal assets and his family. He did not want to jeopardise the family home and his family members should something go wrong.

His final concern was having a costly and complicated structure that he would find difficult to understand and manage. He was very comfortable handling his current business affairs as a sole trader and was concerned about all the additional issues he might have to deal with.

With these three concerns in mind, I advised that a company structure would offer the best solution. His turnover projections were below the $2 million small business threshold and therefore he could take advantage of the 28.5 per cent company tax rate. If his turnover continued to grow and exceeded the $2 million threshold, he would still benefit from the 30 per cent company tax rate as opposed to the top-tier individual income tax rate of 49 per cent. This saved him over $70,000 in income tax, which effectively funded a full-time supervisor he employed to help him manage his jobs.

This structure also enabled him to protect his family home. Because the family home was in his and his wife's names, we appointed his adult son as the sole director of the company, thus separating ownership of the assets. This solution had the added benefit of not having to transfer the title of the family home between family members, saving money and eliminating the potential complications should there be any family disputes in the future.

Finally, he was very comfortable with the affordable setup costs of a company and the ease with which it could be managed. While it added one additional tax return at the end of the financial year, the cost of preparing the additional return paled into insignificance against the benefits he received and still today continues to.

WHAT SHOULD YOU BE THINKING ABOUT?

So how do you know which structure you need? There are a number of factors to consider when choosing a structure. Some of the key ones are as follows:

- Asset protection

- Tax minimisation

- Control

- Active or passive income

- Cost

- Ease of administration

- Adaptability

- Succession planning

Generally, the structure should take care of itself, as long as all the factors have been considered. So let's take a closer look at those factors.

Asset protection

The first consideration when choosing your business structure is how you can best protect your personal assets, like your home, your car and so on.

Running a business can make your personal assets vulnerable in a number of ways – should you ever get sued by a client, partner or supplier; when you need to borrow money from a bank or other trading partners; and should something happen to you as the owner.

When it comes to liability, there are a range of reasons why you might get sued. Knowingly or unknowingly, you might not complete work in the manner a client was expecting, you might violate employment laws, you might violate terms of a partnership agreement and more. If a court finds you guilty, you will likely need to pay a financial sum to the other party involved in the case.

Where does the money come from?

This is where your business structure comes in. First, it's important to adequately insure against the possibility of being sued. However, if that is not possible, or if the sum you have insured yourself for is less than the payment you need to make, your personal assets could be vulnerable.

Instances where insurance protection may not be possible are when you, the business owner and/or your employees, are found to be in fault for specific wrong-doing. As a business owner, you would not likely be performing any deliberate act which would cause damage to another party. If, for some reason, this occurs, insurance will not protect you. Similarly, should your employees cause such damage, you will likely be liable. You need to vigilant to ensure as best you can that these occurrences do not eventuate.

Dealing with unscrupulous individuals is also likely to limit your protection, as are conflicts of interest. In these scenarios, physical damage does not have to result for you to possibly find yourself in hot water. Ensure that you and your company's ethics are always above reproach.

Acts of nature can also limit your protection so, where possible, you should incorporate into your contracts relevant clauses which do not hold your company, your employees and yourself liable for such acts.

All in all, this area can become a legal minefield, so I strongly recommend you have in place all relevant insurances for you and your business.

If you run your business as a sole trader, you and the business are considered to be a single entity. This means that, if the business is sued, your personal assets are fair game. In order to pay the mandated sum, you might be forced to sell your home, and any other assets you have.

By contrast, if your business structure was a company or a trust, that is considered to be a separate entity. As a result, your house is not likely to be at risk.

Similarly, if your business is likely to borrow money, whether it is from a bank or other trading partners, it is important that it has enough assets to satisfy these creditors should you be unable to pay a loan.

Again, if you and your business are a single entity, you might be required to sell your personal assets to pay back your creditors. By contrast, if your business is in a separate structure, assets owned by the business may need to be sold off to pay any debts, but your personal assets will be protected.

Keep in mind that, depending upon your actions and also the bank's conditions of lending, complete asset protection may not be able to be achieved. The government and the banking industry are continually putting measures in place to try and limit your ability to be shielded by separate business structures.

The third area to consider when it comes to asset protection is how you can protect your assets should something happen to you. What will happen if you get sick or injured? What will happen if you pass away? What will happen if you divorce and your spouse makes a claim, or if adult children want control of the business?

Other than having all your personal health and life insurances in place, the type of entity you operate your business in could impact what happens to your business.

If you can no longer operate the business, for example, the type of entity will determine how ownership and/or control of the business can be passed to other family members without triggering tax or incurring excess costs. A trust may provide the ease of transfer without triggering tax and costs, whereas a transfer of the assets in a company will incur capital gains tax if there is an increase in value in the business.

In the case of divorce, you may wish to protect your business interests from your estranged spouse. If you operate your business in a company and you and/or spouse hold shares in that company, then protection may not be possible. Should you hold this business in trust and there are a number of beneficiaries, none of whom are presently entitled, then protection would be more likely.

Finally, just as you want to protect your personal assets from your business, you should also try and protect the assets of your business from your own personal assets.

For example, if you are starting a property development and you also own and operate a painting business, you will want to make sure you protect the assets of the property development from claims of the creditors of the painting business.

Your options for structuring the new property development business include running it as a sole trader, in partnership, as a company or as a trust.

As an individual, because you are also the sole director and shareholder of your painting business, your property development would be totally exposed and therefore vulnerable to the creditors of your painting business. This option would not be ideal.

In a partnership, your vulnerability will depend on the partner and whether your partner has ownership of any significant assets. For instance, if you form a partnership with your spouse and the family home is in your spouse's name (because you wanted to protect that against the painting business), you would still be exposed and vulnerable to the creditors of the painting business for your share of the property. In addition, your spouse is now also exposed. Again, this option would not be ideal.

Let's consider a company using the same set of assumptions. You would need to determine who the director/s and shareholder/s would be. If it was you, you would be potentially exposed via director's personal guarantees. If it was your spouse, the family home would be exposed. So, unless you can make someone else the director, this option also would not be ideal.

The final option is a trust. When considering the same set of circumstances, a trust is definitely an option. Earlier in this chapter, in the section 'What are your options', I explained briefly what a trust is and the benefit of a discretionary trust. To elaborate further, the trustee of the trust is charged with the responsibility of administering and managing the assets of the trust. If the trustee was an individual, then that individual trustee's personal assets could be exposed. If, however, that trustee was a company, then the company would be exposed. The benefit of the company is that it will not own any assets and be limited to its shares, for example $10. That is the extent of its exposure. Therefore, a discretionary trust structure (with a corporate trustee) will provide the best form of protection against your painting business and also against your personal home. In addition to the above benefit, the trust does not have any individual beneficiary who is presently entitled to the assets of the trust and therefore no creditor has access to the assets of the trust. The trustee controls the trust and as such no beneficiary has a fixed entitlement. This is definitely the best option in this example.

As you can see, asset protection can be a very sensitive issue and is one that needs your utmost attention.

Tax minimisation

When it comes to structuring your business to minimise tax, there are two areas to consider – your business's taxable income and any potential for Capital Gains Tax (CGT).

If your business derives a taxable income, then minimising income tax will be an important factor when choosing your business structure.

You want to ensure that any profit generated by your business is taxed at the lowest possible rate. This can be done by ensuring that individual tax rates and tax-free thresholds are taken advantage of, and that any additional income is taxed at a corporate rate.

At the time of writing, income tax rates in Australia are as follows:

Taxable income	Tax on this income[1]
$0–$18,200	Nil
$18,201–$37,000	19c for each $1 over $18,200
$37,00 –$87,000	$3,572 plus 32.5c for each $1 over $37,000
$87,001–$180,000	$19,822 plus 37c for each $1 over $87,000
$180,001 and over	$54,232 plus 45c for every $1 over $180,000

As I described earlier, different structures have different treatments of tax. If you are a sole trader, all profit earned by the business will be counted towards your personal income and taxed at the rates above. The same goes for partnerships, though the profit would be divided between the partners.

---

1   Note that these rates do not include the two per cent Medicare levy, or the Temporary Budget Repair Levy – payable at a rate of two per cent for incomes over $180,000.

Profits generated by companies, on the other hand, are taxed at a rate of either 28.5 per cent or 30 per cent, depending on their aggregated turnover. *Please note there is current legislation pending to reduce the 28.5% company tax rate to 27.5% for small business entities.*

Using the figures above, the percentage of income tax you pay increases as your income does, reaching a total of 30 per cent at $180,000 in income (total tax paid of $54,232 ÷ total income of $180,000 = 30%). After this, the percentage increases with every additional dollar earned. This means businesses making over $180,000 in profit can pay a lower percentage of tax than they would have otherwise if they use a company structure. You can also gain tax benefits if your income is less than $180,000 where you could pay yourself $87,000 as a salary or wage and leave $93,000 of income in the company to pay tax at the corporate rate. In this example, you would save either nine or 10.5 per cent tax.

When it comes to trusts, the income is distributed to beneficiaries and is then recorded as a part of their taxable income. As you can choose how much income goes to each beneficiary, you can maximise your tax benefit by paying more income to beneficiaries who are in lower income brackets, and benefit from lower tax rates.

Finally, SMSFs pay a flat tax rate of 15 per cent on the net earnings, including concessional contributions. This structure is the most tax efficient, however, it is also the structure with the most restrictions in regard to operating a business, as stated earlier.

Note that the government is continually putting in place measures to reduce the tax benefits of certain structures depending on the type of business you run and how you run that business. For example, contractors in the building industry are now facing the likelihood that the ATO will not grant them an individual ABN if the ATO believes that they are effectively operating as an employee contracting to one employer for only their labour services. Instead, a business operation in the eyes of the ATO is one where you contract to two or more employers and when you supply your own plant and equipment and/or materials.

The second area to consider when it comes to tax minimisation is Capital Gains Tax (CGT).

If your business derives income that is considered capital, then planning to minimise CGT is important.

Income that would be considered capital is the profit made when you sell an asset. Under that simple definition, property development would be considered capital. Unfortunately, it is not that simple, as the ATO has introduced significant legislation in this area. For example, if you undergo a property development and your intention is to make a profit by selling the developed properties at completion, the ATO now considers such an activity as income, not capital.

So, what might they consider capital? If we take the example above but change the intention from selling the developed properties at completion to renting the developed properties for a period of time before, then selling them at some time in the future, this scenario would be considered capital at the time of sale of the rental properties.

The ATO provides a tax incentive for you to hold on to assets for a period of at least 12 months, where they will give you a 50 per cent CGT discount on the profit on the sale of the properties.

The other main activity that would be considered capital, and one that is generally not even considered when setting up a structure, is the sale of your business. If your intention is to build value in your business and sell it for a significant profit at some point in the future, then CGT should be a major consideration.

Structuring your business so that you can get access to both the CGT

50 per cent discount and various small business concessions is important if you plan to generate income that is considered capital.

So which structure should you choose? The only structure which is not entitled to the 50 per cent CGT discount is a company. Therefore, all of the other structures are valid options for accessing the CGT discount along with other small business concessions.

However, while a company cannot access the CGT discount, there is a loophole. If you operate your business in a company structure you can benefit from the CGT discount if you sell your shares in the company, rather than selling the business and retaining the company. The shareholder then becomes the seller and if the shareholder is you (individual) or a trust you are connected with, then you can access the CGT discount. You need to be aware, though, that a purchaser may not wish to acquire the shares in your company as it may not suit their requirements.

You may also minimise CGT by conducting your business through an existing entity with available capital losses. For example, if you have an existing trust that has capital losses from a previous investment that was sold at a loss, this can be offset against a future capital gain, thus reducing the total profit and the tax you'll need to pay as a result.

It is important to also consider the other taxes that affect your business, including payroll tax, stamp duty and land tax. Other costs include workers' compensation, superannuation guarantee contributions and leave entitlements.

Control

Ownership and control are not the same thing. It is important you understand the difference and how it may impact you moving forward.

Control is when a person, or group of people, have a controlling interest (more than 50 per cent) across two or more businesses. Control is not limited by the type of structure that you operate in, meaning the different businesses could be operated as a sole trader, partnership, trust or company. Therefore, you cannot escape these provisions just by setting up a new company or trust, unless there is a different person in control (meaning, someone else is the director or trustee).

The key distinction between ownership and control is that the owner and the person/people in control may not be the same under some of the structures we have discussed. For instance, in a business run as a sole trader, the business owner also has the controlling interest in the business, so the same person has both ownership and control. In a company, on the other hand, the business is owned by the shareholders, whereas the business is controlled by the director.

Structure	Ownership	Control	Same/Different
Sole trader	Sole trader	Sole trader	Same
Partnership	Partners	Partners	Same
Company	Shareholders	Directors	Can be different entities
Trust	Beneficiaries	Trustee	Can be different entities

In companies and trusts, the owner and the person/people in control may or may not be the same.

For instance, Scabbit Builders Pty. Ltd. is run and managed by Brett, who has been appointed the Director of the company. Brett's wife, Kristen, assists with the business when she can and she holds all the shares in the company. They own their family home and the title lists Kristen as the sole owner. This structure has Brett, the director of the company, as the person in control, while Kristen, the shareholder, is the owner of the company. In addition, we have the added benefit of protecting the family home as there is no responsibility attached to Kristen as she does not control the company and therefore does not have any liability should there be any legal of financial disputes.

It is common in smaller businesses that the person or people who own the business also control the business. In the vast majority of cases it will depend on the owner's family network and personal circumstances. The point to note here is that there is a distinction and understanding that could be of assistance when it comes to running more than one business and the possibility of minimising taxes and costs.

Active or passive income

The type of income you earn will also influence your structure, and is linked to the tax minimisation strategies you use. Your income might be active, passive or both.

Active income comes from a trading business, such as a building company, while passive income comes from investment activities, like having an investment property that earns rental income.

If your business is generating active income, your priority will be minimising income tax, as discussed earlier. You will likely also want to access CGT small business concessions on the eventual sale of the business, unless your intention is to pass it down to family.

If your structure is to derive passive income, you are likely to place more importance on the minimisation of CGT liability in the sale of the investment.

While it's possible to have a business that will derive both passive and active income, it is often advisable to separate the two activities in two separate structures. First, this enables you protect the assets of one business against the assets of the other. Second, having separate structures for the different income types will allow you to minimise tax, as you can choose the most appropriate structure for each income type.

Cost

All structures will incur a cost, whether that is the cost of setting up the structure, registrations, ongoing renewals and the cost of tax and accounting.

Generally, the more complex the structure, the higher the cost will be to set it up and maintain. Other factors affecting the cost of ongoing maintenance include the nature and size of the business, the complexity of the business transactions, the quality of records kept by the business and whether accounting systems are used. The size of the accounting or law firm involved in the preparation of the work will also impact costs.

Following are some indicative costs for each of the entities (all figures current at the time of writing).

	Individual	Partnership	Company	Trust
Setup	$0	$500–$1,000 (starting cost for a partnership agreement)	ASIC registration: $469 If you register online: $200–$300 If a tax agent registers you: $1,200–$1,500 (including ABN and TFN registration) If a shareholder's agreement is required: $500–$1,000.	If you register online: $200–$300 If you require a corporate trustee: $469 If a tax agent registers you: $2,000–$2,500 (including corporate trustee, ABN and TFN registration) NB: Some states also have a stamp duty on trust deeds.
Business name registration	$80 for three years via ASIC	$80 for three years via ASIC	No need for separate registration	No need for separate registration
ABN registration	If you register: $0 If a tax agent registers you: $150–$250	If you register: $0 If a tax agent registers you: $200–$300	If you register: $0 If a tax agent registers you: $200–$300	If you register: $0 If a tax agent registers you: $200–$300
Annual tax return	$500–$750 (Based on a small business with good internal accounting system)	$750–$1,000 (Based on a small business with good internal accounting system)	$1,500–$2,000 (Based on a small business with good internal accounting system)	$1,500–$2,000 (Based on a small business with good internal accounting system)
Annual ASIC renewal			$249 on anniversary of incorporation	

When considering costs, be sure that you keep the longer-term benefits in mind rather than taking a short-term view because what may seem like a cost burden now may save you thousands of dollars in the future. I would strongly recommend seeking professional advice from an accountant and lawyer for every aspect of structuring of your business.

Ease of administration

A complex structure that involves various layers will have more compliance issues attached to it, than a simpler structure.

For example, a structure consisting of a company and a unit trust with two discretionary trusts as unit holders may provide the ideal structure for a smaller business that will also make some investments. However, such a structure requires that four entities be accounted for in addition to the business owner's individual returns. In addition, trading between the structures will add an extra layer of complexity.

By contrast, if your business is held in a single unit trust and you are the sole beneficiary, it will be far simpler to manage. However, you may not experience the same benefits when it comes to tax minimisation and asset protection.

Where does this leave you when choosing a structure? Do you just leave it to your accountant? Do you just pick whatever sounds like the right thing?

Unfortunately, there is no one-structure-fits-all-scenario. Therefore, your particular circumstances need to be taken into account.

Trading businesses generating income are best kept simple. Remember, the KISS (Keep It Simple Stupid) philosophy I raised at the beginning of the book? This is where it comes to the fore. As a general rule, the smaller the business the more likely a sole trader or partnership structure may be the best option. The larger the business (and depending on access to family members who can be beneficiaries), the more likely a company or trust structure would best suit.

The complexity tends to become a reality when there are business partners and there is an investment or asset holding in addition to the trading entity.

If you own an asset or plan to purchase an asset in connection with your business, you would be best advised to hold that asset in a separate entity, whether or not you have partners. Without partners, a simple discretionary trust may suit your requirements so you can access CGT concessions. With partners, an additional entity, such as a unit trust, may best suit your requirements, with each partner owning their share of units in their own discretionary trust.

Finally, keep in mind that simple or straightforward structures will enable easier access to borrowing from financial institutions. Banks have a tendency to shy away from structures that they do not fully understand. That is not to say that it is not possible with a more complex structure, however, it is something that you need to be consider before finalising your structure.

Ability to adapt

Having a structure that can provide flexibility can be of great assistance as your business grows and changes. Changing market conditions and changing legislative provisions can require that a structure be altered, whether in a small way or completely.

You may also wish to introduce new equity partners at some time in the future. This should be considered at the time of setting up the structure, as some structures will not allow such a change, such as discretionary trusts. There are no fixed entitlements in a discretionary trust and all beneficiaries are nominated when the trust is established. Any change to beneficiaries will cause a resettlement to the trust thereby incurring additional tax and costs for the changes required.

If you would prefer a trust structure, based on the other benefits, a unit trust may be a better option as it allows you to admit additional equity partners through the issuing or transfer of units. For example, if Tim and Peter each owned 60 units in a unit trust and they wanted to give their friend Andrew an equal share of the business, they would have the option to either issue him with 60 units or each sell 20 units to him to equalise the ownership at a third of the business.

Similarly, a company structure would be also suitable in such circumstances where existing shares could be transferred or new shares issued in the same way as the units in the example above.

Succession planning

None of us like to think of a time when we won't be around anymore, but this needs to be considered up front so you can plan for it effectively.

Whether you plan to sell your business on your retirement, leave your share to your partners or hand it on to your children will influence the type of structure you choose. It's also important to consider what you would like to happen should you pass away while you are still holding the reins. You need to consider who will control the income and assets of the structure and how this control could be changed, if required.

If you plan to sell, will you sell the entire business or just its assets?

Before answering that question, you need to ask yourself whether your business has a value in the open marketplace. Many business owners run their businesses and generate good incomes. Unfortunately, when it comes time to pack up the toolkit, their businesses do not have real value to anyone else because they themselves are 'the business'. The business cannot run without them, hence there is no value. A harsh reality, but definitely one that is better knowing now rather than later.

If you find yourself in this position, you may be able to sell your business's assets, but will likely struggle to sell the business itself. If, on the other hand, your business could run effectively without you in it, you have options.

If you have a company structure you have the option of selling the shares in the company or just the business interest the company operates. If you sell the shares in the company, then the capital gain or loss sits with the shareholder that sells the shares, which could be an individual or a trust, depending on how the company was structured when incorporated. That shareholder will need to report the capital in their tax return. If the company sells the business interest, on the other hand, then it is the company that has made a capital gain and loss, and it would need to report that capital gain or loss accordingly.

If the business is operated under a trust, on the other hand, it would be difficult to sell the interests in the trust. Trusts are established for the benefit of its beneficiaries, which are generally family members when it comes to discretionary trusts (the most common trust structures established for business).

If you are operating your business in a discretionary trust, or planning to do so, please consider your succession planning as, if you are likely to sell your business to external parties, you will likely be selling the business assets, rather than the interest in the trust.

If your intention is to pass the business to your children, a trust can be a cost effective and easy option, as your children are already beneficiaries of your trust irrespective of whether they are named beneficiaries or not. It is standard in discretionary trusts that your children, along with siblings, parents and so on, are all unnamed beneficiaries. There is no obligation to distribute any funds to them at any stage, but the option is there for you should your circumstances warrant it (such as when your net business income is at a high level and you wish to save tax by utilising as many of your family members lower tax rate thresholds).

Another consideration is small business CGT concessions on the sale of your business or its assets. When it comes to CGT, an individual and/or trust is able to access the CGT 50 per cent discount while a company cannot, therefore this should be kept in mind when considering succession planning and choosing your business structure. If your business is considered to be a small business entity (with turnover of less than $2 million), additional CGT concessions – like the 50 per cent active asset reduction and the $500,000 retirement concession – will play a significant part in your decision.

SUMMARY

You will notice there are a number of elements you need to consider when setting up the structure for your business venture. Your specific circumstances will determine which structure will be best suited to your needs. In addition, what may seem the perfect fit today may not be the perfect fit in the future. The one thing you need to know is that choosing the wrong structure could be very costly, so you don't want to be paying taxes if it is not necessary just because you've chosen the wrong structure.

CHAPTER 3: STATUTORY

*'It is easy to dodge our responsibilities, but we cannot
dodge the consequences of dodging our responsibilities.'*
— Josiah Charles Stamp

The building and property development industry has its own compliance regulations to ensure all the necessary standards are met.

The Australia Building Codes Board (ABCB) is responsible for developing and managing the national approach to building codes and building materials. Each state or territory of Australia has its own regulations, with many common requirements established by the ABCB.

At a state level, your state building authority requires that, as a builder, you must be a registered building practitioner and use a building contract when work costs more than $5,000. This work includes such things as building a house, renovations, extensions, garages, driveways, demolition and even preparing plans. You must also take out Domestic Building Insurance when the cost of the work reaches a certain level ($16,000 in Victoria or $20,000 in New South Wales, for instance).

You are required to complete your building project to the standard and quality of work required by the building regulations as well as your plans and specifications. If the building project requires a building permit, there are fines that can be levied against you if you carry out that work without a permit.

Meeting these compliance requirements is a must, otherwise approvals will not be granted and/or rectification will be required, which can be a costly exercise. In some cases, it could be your entire profit on a job, or even as much as the total cost of the job. Worse still, you could lose your licences and registrations and, in certain cases, your insurances may not be able to help.

There is no difference when it comes to the financial management of your business.

You need to ensure that all of your statutory compliance is met on time and with complete accuracy. If you don't, you'll be hit with penalties, interest and extra costs to fix the problem.

This is even true in areas that you may believe are simple or straight-forward, such as hiring contractors versus hiring employees. You may think you know the difference, but do you really? To be considered a contractor, certain criteria need to be met:

- They need to have a certain level of control over the work they are performing on a day-to-day basis.

- They are engaged to produce a specific result.

- They have the right to delegate work.

- They bear the commercial risk and responsibility for their work or injury.

- They provide their own tools, equipment and, in some cases, materials.

- They work for you on an as-needs basis, rather than being an integral part of your business.

They may have an ABN, but that in itself is not enough. They may work for you only 80 per cent of their time, but that is also not enough. They may only work for you for a short period of time, such as two months, but that is still not enough to consider them to be considered a contractor.

So let's take a look at the main compliance requirements for your business, and how you can ensure you meet them.

COMPLIANCE REQUIREMENTS

The main compliance requirements you need to be aware of in a building and property development business include tax, superannuation, workers' compensation, payroll tax, land tax and stamp duty.

Tax

There are a number of tax obligations that every business needs to meet.

The first is your obligation to lodge annual tax returns to the ATO, be they as an individual, partnership, company, trust or self-managed superannuation fund.

The second is your obligation to lodge monthly or quarterly activity statements. Activity statements account for your goods and services tax (GST), your pay as you go (PAYG) withholding and your PAYG instalments. The frequency of your activity statements will depend on the turnover of your business (for GST) and the level of your payroll (PAYG). Irrespective of the frequency, the obligation remains the same: lodgement must take place.

Lodging your annual tax return and your monthly or quarterly activity statements can be managed with minimal effort using cloud accounting tools – a must for businesses in today's commercial world. It not only helps with lodging on time, but also making sure you've reported accurately.

Once again, this is an area where cash flow management is important. While lodgement is one key compliance requirement, payment is the other. Ensuring you have accurately captured all relevant income and expenses will ensure the accuracy of reporting. Having done so will help you manage your cash flow position because you will know exactly what is required to make provision for the necessary payments of your tax obligations.

If your activity statement results in an amount payable, this typically suggests that you have received more business income than you have paid business expenses, not including payroll. In this instance, if your cash flow is effectively managed, you should have the funds to make payment. Sounds simple enough, doesn't it? Unfortunately, it can be tempting to utilise some of that excess cash elsewhere and, as a result, be left a little short when payment to the ATO is required. However, if you are monitoring your financial statements on a monthly basis, as discussed in Chapter 1, this will help prevent this from happening.

Meeting these ATO obligations keeps you ahead of the game. There are some non-negotiables in business and the ATO is one of them. The sooner you accept its place in business and the obligation for the lodgement and payment of your compliance requirements, the better off you will be.

Superannuation

The next compliance issue relates to your labour force – superannuation.

The superannuation guarantee scheme requires you to provide a minimum level of superannuation for your employees, currently being 9.5 per cent of their gross pay. If you don't pay the required minimum, you will be liable to pay a *non-deductible* superannuation guarantee charge, which is made up of the superannuation shortfall (the super you should have paid) plus nominal interest of ten per cent plus an administration charge of $20 per quarter per employee.

This might not sound like a significant penalty, but I can assure you that it can quickly add up to be a major financial burden. Not to mention that the ATO does not take too kindly to employers failing their superannuation guarantee charge obligations.

When you employ people on your payroll, it is relatively straightforward to understand your requirement to pay superannuation. What sometimes gets lost or forgotten is the requirement to pay the same 9.5 per cent of gross payments to your subcontractors. Not all your subcontractors would attract this requirement, but those who just supply labour as individuals/ sole traders and those who work predominately for you would.

Why? The answer is that the ATO sees those contractors as employees, particularly if they are not employed to produce a specific result on a specific job or project and they are employed as part of a larger work group to work together to complete that project. In other words, they are no different to the employees on your payroll.

There is no obligation to pay those subcontractors who are employed to perform a specific job, such as roofing contractors, electrical contractors and plumbers. If the transaction is considered to be a business-to-business relationship with another company that supplies labour and materials, then the obligation for superannuation does not exist.

Understanding the difference between the two will ensure you comply accordingly. More importantly, with this knowledge, you may seek to employ subcontractors on a different basis moving forward so as to not impose additional obligations on your business.

Workers' compensation

A requirement from day one of employing a labour force is to ensure that they are covered for any injury caused relating to their employment with your business.

Workers' compensation applies in a similar manner to superannuation. If the labour, be it under an employee relationship or as a permanent or semi-permanent subcontractor, is considered to be an employee relationship in the eyes of the industrial relations and tax law regime, then workers' compensation is required to be paid.

You can pay it quarterly or yearly in advance and it is based on your estimate of what your rateable remuneration will be for that financial year. Should your estimate be higher, you will be entitled to a refund that will usually take the form of a reduction of the next year's premium. Should your estimate be lower, you will be required to pay the excess at the end of the financial year.

You have a requirement to lodge an annual Certificate of Remuneration to confirm what your actual payments to employees, directors, contractors and apprentices were for the financial year, including payment of superannuation. On this annual certificate, you are also required to estimate the following year's total payment to the above labour force. This estimate then forms the basis for the premium you will be required to pay for the upcoming financial year.

Just like with superannuation, determining how you engage the services of subcontractors will have an impact on your workers' compensation payments.

While there is a financial impact of deciding whether your labour force will be employees or external contractors, the issue of control may be just as important, if not more so. As explained earlier, you have total control and direction over employees in terms of what they do, how they do it and when they do it. When it comes to external contractors, they control how and when they perform the work, and even who performs the work, within the specific requirements of the job. They can delegate to their employees or subcontractors, and their methods could well differ to your own. While you may lose some control, you do benefit from not having to direct and manage the work, given you have confidence in the contractor you have employed to perform the work.

Payroll tax

Should your total employee workforce reach a certain threshold, you will be required to pay payroll tax. The threshold of each state of Australia differs as follows:

- Victoria: $575,000

- New South Wales: $750,000

- Australian Capital Territory: $2,000,000

- Queensland: $1,100,000

- South Australia: $600,000

- Western Australia: $850,000

- Northern Territory: $1,500,000

- Tasmania: $1,250,000

Depending on your particular building and property development operation, this could have a material impact.

Typically, in a property development project the labour force would be external to your business and therefore would not impact you at all. However, in a building operation, this is something you may need to monitor, particularly if your operation fluctuates depending on the projects you have year to year.

While fairly straightforward, payroll tax is something that has the potential to sneak up on you, particularly if you have not been exposed to it in the past.

One way to monitor this is to record your monthly wage bill. If you keep an eye on it at regular intervals, there should be no surprises.

Land tax

In a business where you hold land for investment purposes, you need to be mindful of any land tax implications. Land tax is essentially a tax for holding land for investment or business purposes. This includes property where you operate your business or property you lease to another entity to operate their business. Land tax is not paid on your principal place of residence.

From the point of view of your building business, an example is an office or warehouse you may have bought to run your building business from. When referring to a property development business, an example is a complex of five townhouses you built and developed and now lease for rental purposes.

The greater the value of land you hold, the more land tax you will pay as the percentage rate of tax increases as the value increases, much like the individual income tax rates.

Land tax is payable in all Australian states and the ACT but not in the Northern Territory, and it is levied against the registered land owner, except in the ACT where it applies to all residential properties that are rented or are owned by a company or trust.

The state authorities calculate the land tax based on the rateable vale of the land, which appears on your local rates notices, and multiplies it by the percentage rate of tax based on the total value.

I've listed land tax rates for investment properties at the time of writing, not including any concession policies, below.

Victoria

Taxable value of land	Rate of tax
$0 to $250,000	Nil
$250,000 to $600,000	$275 plus 0.2% of amount > $250,000
$600,000 to $1,000,000	$975 plus 0.5% of amount > $600,000
$1,000,000 to $1,800,000	$2,975 plus 0.8% of amount > $1,000,000
$1,800,000 to $3,000,000	$9,375 plus 1.3% of amount > $1,800,000
$3,000,000+	$24,975 plus 2.25% of amount > $3,000,000

New South Wales

Taxable value of land	Rate of tax
Threshold	
$0 to $549,000	$100 plus 1.6% up to premium threshold
Premium threshold	
$3,357,000+	$45,028 for the first $3,357,000 then 2% over that

Queensland

Taxable value of land	Rate of tax
$0 to $599,999	Nil
$600,0000 to $999,999	$500 plus 1 cent for each $1 more than $600,000
$1,000,000 to $2,999,999	$4,500 plus 1.65 cents for each $1 more than $1,000,000
$3,000,000 to $4,999,999	$37,500 plus 1.25 cents for each $1 more than $3,000,000
$5,000,000+	$62,500 plus 1.75 cents for each $1 more than $5,000,000
$3,000,000+	$24,975 plus 2.25% of amount > $3,000,000

South Australia

Taxable value of land	Rate of tax
$0 to $332,000	Nil
$332,001 to $609,000	$0.50 for every $100 or part of $100 above $332,000
$609,001 to $886,000	$1385 plus $1,65 for every $100 or part of $100 above $609,000
$886,001 to $1,108,000	$5955.50 plus $2.40 for every $100 or part of $100 above $886,000
$1,108,000+	$11283.50 plus $3.70 for every $100 or part of $100 above $1,108,000
$3,000,000+	$24,975 plus 2.25% of amount > $3,000,000

Western Australia

Taxable value of land	Rate of tax
$0 to $300,000	Nil
$300,001 to $420,000	Flat rate of $300
$420,000 to $1,000,000	$300 plus 0.25 cents for each $1 more than $420,000
$1,000,000 to $1,800,000	$1,750 plus 0.90 cents for each $1 more than $1,000,000
$1,800,000 to $5,000,000	$8,950 plus 1.80 cents for each $1 more than $1,800,000
$5,000,000 to $11,000,000	$66,550 plus 2.00 cents for each $1 more than $5,000,000
$11,000,000+	$186,550 plus 2.67 cents for each $1 more than $11,000,000

Tasmania

Taxable value of land	Rate of tax
$0 to $24,999	Nil
$25,000 to $349,999	$50 plus 0.55% of value above $25,000
$350,000+	$1,837.50 plus 1.5% of value above $350,000

Australian Capital Territory

Taxable value of land	Rate of tax
$0 to $75,000	$1,090 plus 0.41%
$75,001 to $150,000	$1,090 plus 0.48% of amount above $75,000
$150,001 to $275,000	$1,090 plus 0.61% of amount above $150,000
$275,001+	$1,090 plus 1.23% of amount above $275,000

Following on from the examples above, if your building company's office or warehouse is valued at $800,000 and you are based in Victoria, land tax is calculated as $975 (for the first $600,000) plus 0.5 per cent on the additional $200,000, which is an extra $1,000. Therefore, the total land tax payable on your office or warehouse is $1,975. The same property would cost you $4,116 in New South Wales or $2,500 in Queensland.

If you had a property development business with five townhouses with a total value of $3,500,000, the land tax payable on $3,000,000 in Victoria is $24,975, plus 2.25 per cent on the additional $500,000, which is an extra $11,250. Therefore, the total land tax payable on your five townhouses is $36,225. The same development would cost you $47,316 in New South Wales and $43,750 in Queensland.

As mentioned earlier when discussing tax minimisation in structures, you need to be mindful of the government's grouping provisions. These provisions dictate that if the same person is the ultimate owner, irrespective of the structure, they will be grouped together and land tax payable at a higher rate.

Stamp duty

When you purchase land or property, you are required to pay stamp duty on the purchase. Stamp duty rates vary depending on the price of the property as well as the state in which the property is located.

I've listed stamp duty rates for investment properties at the time of writing, not including any concession policies, below.

Victoria

Purchase/value amount	Duty payable
$0 to $25,000	1.4% of dutiable value
$25,001 to $130,000	$350 + 2.4% of dutiable value over $25,000
$130,001 to $440,000	$2,870 + 5% of dutiable value over $130,000
$440,001 to $550,000	$18,370 + 6% of dutiable value over $440,000
$550,001 to $960,000	$2,870 + 6% of dutiable value over $130,000
Over $960,000	5.5% of dutiable value

NSW

Purchase/value amount	Duty payable
$0 to $14,000	$1.25 for every $100 or part of the value
$14,001 to $30,000	$175 + $1.50 for every $100 after $14,001
$30,001 to $80,000	$415 + $1.75 for every $100 after $30,001
$80,001 to $300,000	$1,290 + $3.50 for every $100 after $80,001
$300,001 to $1 million	$8,990 + $4.50 for every $100 after $300,001
Over $1 million	$40,490 + $5.50 for every $100 after $1,000,001
Premium property duty: over $3 million	$150,490 + $7 for every $100 after $3,000,001

Queensland

Purchase/value amount	Duty payable
$0 to $5,000	No stamp duty payable
$5,001 to $105,000	1.5% of dutiable value over $5,000
$105,001 to $480,000	$1,500 + 3.5% of dutiable value over $105,000
$480,001 to $980,000	$14,625 + 4.5% of dutiable value over $480,000
Over $980,000	$37,125 + 5.25% of dutiable value over $980,000

South Australia

Purchase/value amount	Duty payable
$0 to $12,000	1% of dutiable value
$12,001 to $30,000	$120 + 2% of dutiable value over $12,000
$30,001 to $50,000	$480 + 3% of dutiable value over $30,000
$50,001 to $100,000	$1,080 + 3.5% of dutiable value over $50,000
$100,001 to $200,000	$2,830 + 4% of dutiable value over $100,000
$200,001 to $250,000	$6,830 + 4.25% of dutiable value over $200,000
$250,001 to $300,000	$8,955 + 4.75% of dutiable value over $250,000
$300,001 to $500,000	$11,330 + 5% of dutiable value over $300,000
Over $500,000	$21,330 + 5.5% of dutiable value over $500,000

Western Australia

Purchase/value amount	Duty payable
$0 to $120,000	1.9% of dutiable value
$120,001 to $150,000	$2,280 + 2.85% of dutiable value over $120,000
$150,001 to $360,000	$3,135 + 3.8% of dutiable value over $150,000
$360,001 to $725,000	$11,115 + 4.75% of dutiable value over $360,000
Over $725,000	$28,435 + 5.15% of dutiable value over $725,000

Tasmania

Purchase/value amount	Duty payable
$0 to $1,300	$20
$1,301 to $10,000	1.5% of dutiable value
$10,001 to $30,000	$150 + 2% of dutiable value over $10,000
$30,001 to $75,000	$550 + 2.5% of dutiable value over $30,000
$75,001 to $150,000	$1,675 + 3% of dutiable value over $75,000
$150,001 to $225,000	$3,925 + 3.5% of dutiable value over $150,000
Over $225,000	$6,550 + 4% of dutiable value over $225,000

ACT

Purchase/value amount	Duty payable
$0 to $100,000	2% of dutiable value or $20, whichever is greater
$100,001 to $200,000	$2,000 + 3.5% of dutiable value over $100,000
$200,001 to $300,000	$5,500 + 4% of dutiable value over $200,000
$300,001 to $500,000	$9,500 + 5.5% of dutiable value over $300,000
$500,001 to $1,000,000	$20,500 + 5.75% of dutiable value over $500,000
Over $1 million	$49,250 + 6.75% of dutiable value over $1 million

Northern Territory

Purchase/value amount	Duty payable
$0 to $525,000	See above formula
$525,001 to $3,000,000	4.95% of dutiable value
Over $3 million	5.45% of dutiable value

Regardless of your state, stamp duty adds up and is something you should be aware of when costing any acquisition. There are exemptions or concessions for first home buyers and purchasing property off the plan, however, these are not likely to come into effect in your business.

SUMMARY

In summary, there are many statutory compliance obligations placed upon you in your building and property development business. Being aware of these is the first step. Being set up to account for these is the second. Knowledge is power but management is success.

CHAPTER 4: SYSTEMS

'Step by step and the thing is done.'
– Charles Atlas

You have spent some valuable time re-shaping, re-cultivating and re-invigorating your business.

You have created a strategic plan to help you achieve your business goals. You have laid a solid foundation for your business by setting up the right structure. You understand your statutory compliance requirements.

Now it's time to get down to money management.

Good financial systems need to be in place to help you manage your business. They will assist in monitoring your financial situation as you move towards your goals, they will ensure you have enough money in the bank to meet your expenses, and will keep you on top of your statutory requirements.

Which systems do you need? At a high level, you will need to look at managing your cash flow, managing your financing and troubleshooting any problems.

MANAGING CASH FLOW

One of the most important aspects of running a business is to ensure you have adequate cash flow to meet all of your financial obligations. Cash is the lifeblood of your business and ensures you stay afloat. Once you are securely afloat, you can then sail towards your destination. (Maybe with a nice refreshment in hand and the people you care about sitting beside you.)

Unfortunately, most business owners tend to focus on profits rather than cash flow, and this is where most cash flow problems begin.

Put simply, there are two sides to your cash flow:

1. Money you receive from your clients for work performed.

2. Money you pay out to workers, suppliers, the ATO and others.

One of the biggest killers to your business cash flow is slow paying customers. It is great to have lots of customers, however, if they are not paying you on time (or at all), that will make it very difficult for you to pay your bills. Your employees, subcontractors and suppliers must all be paid on time, but if your customers aren't paying you, where is the money going to come from?

The second silent killer is your commitments to the ATO. Depending on the size of your business, you will have to pay the ATO for your GST and PAYG obligations either monthly or quarterly. Many business owners still continue to overlook this critical obligation. Whether that is because they don't want to admit they owe anything to the ATO or simply over commit their funds elsewhere, this is a problem. After your workers, the ATO should be your top financial priority. It is one organisation that you do not want to get on the wrong side of.

The third silent killer is over committing expenditure. The way you manage your stock of materials is important. The vast majority of material supplies are readily available and therefore there should be no reason to buy extra 'just in case! The same goes for equipment. While we tend to want to have every piece of equipment that we could possibly ever need, that is not a sensible approach, particularly if there are certain items that would just end up sitting in the warehouse gathering dust. In addition to that, we tend to want the best of everything, and sometimes just because 'the other guys have one! Neither of these are smart business decisions.

It is possible to be making a profit, yet still experiencing cash flow problems. A simple example is when you are generating sales, which increase your profits, but you are not collecting the money and therefore your sales revenue is not the same as your cash inflow. It goes without saying that it's no good completing a job if you don't actually receive the money for it.

Having said that, I am sure you do receive the money at some point in time, but the timing of the receipt is very important. Why? As I discussed last chapter, you have financial commitments to make to the ATO, not to mention to your employees, contractors, suppliers and so on. If you are not collecting sales receipts on your agreed terms, then you will find it difficult to meet those commitments and you could potentially find yourself in severe financial difficulty.

Simply, making more money will not solve your problems if cash flow management is the problem. So it's important to establish strategies to make sure that you have enough cash in the business to operate on a day-to-day basis without facing any sort of cash crisis.

Creating a cash flow forecast

It's essential that you take the time to sit down and map out a plan to get control of your money. That means knowing where, when, how and why it is coming in and going out.

We already addressed your historical cash flow in your strategy (Chapter 1) – the next area to consider is your cash flow forecast for the next 12 months.

The cash flow forecast is a detailed report that shows the predicted movement of your cash position. To create this, you need to understand not only what level of sales and expenditure you are likely to generate, but also the timing of it. This timing determines your cash position at any point in time.

Creating a cash flow forecast is critical for you to be able to manage your cash flow and make sure your business meets all its financial obligations (and, most importantly, leaves you with some cash in your pocket). After all, as an ambitious business owner you are in business to make some money for yourself and improve your own lifestyle, not everyone else's.

To create your cash flow forecast, start with your fixed expenditure. These are those expenses that must be paid on a weekly, monthly, quarterly or yearly basis. These can go directly into your forecast without too much thought.

For a free copy of my Cash Flow template, go to www.adpartners.com.au/cashflow.

The next area to consider is your sales/income. Unfortunately, these areas are not fixed, and neither are the direct variable expenses attached to them. You might not know the exact number of projects you'll be working on over the next 12 months, or the scope of those projects, which makes it difficult to predict your income and expenses like the materials and labour required for those jobs.

A secondary complication is timing – not only do you not know when these projects might take place (and when the direct variable expenses have to be paid), you also can't guarantee that the client will pay you exactly when you want.

Forecasting the timing and dollar value of your sales will depend on both historical and future factors. Some historical factors include how long you have been in business, how stable or predictable it has been, whether your business is growing or shrinking, the size of your operation and what's been happening in the building and property market. Some future factors are whether the recent trend will continue (up or down), whether you are planning to do anything in particular to generate more business or win some large contracts (which would likely give you a fairly predictable outlook), whether you are planning to employ more workers or branch out into other areas.

You can see that there are a number of things that you need to consider and, the more you do, the better you will understand what is happening in your business and the market. The more you know your market needs, the more you can focus on providing exactly that.

Once you have put your projections in place, the next step is analysing what the cash flow forecast is telling you (you may be surprised).

Whether that is the amount and timing of sales or the amount and timing of certain expenses, your forecast will give you a clear picture of what the next 12 months will look like and will likely highlight the areas you need to start focusing on immediately. You will be forced to start thinking about which actions you will take, such as trying to cut down on certain expenses or increasing certain types of revenue streams. You may even decide that you require a capital injection, be it short-term or otherwise. Regardless of what you decide, the benefit of creating a cash flow forecast is that you will be able to make educated decisions because you will have the right information in front of you.

Without this forecast, you just might be guessing. That can be a very dangerous thing because one wrong decision can mean the difference between a healthy profit, completing a project at cost or, worse still, a loss.

It is far more effective to be able to make decisions earlier in the business process and before any potential problems arise. Being proactive, rather than reactive, will substantially increase your likelihood of success.

MAXIMISING YOUR WORKING CAPITAL

One benefit of both reviewing your historical cash flow patterns, as well as creating a cash flow forecast, is being able to make changes that will maximise your working capital.

Working capital is the money you have available to operate your business from day to day. In the building industry, working capital is made up of three key components:

- Payment to suppliers (creditors)

- Work in progress

- Collection from customers (debtors)

How much working capital you have at any one time is dependent on the length of time between you using your cash to purchase materials and pay your labour, and receiving payment for completing a job.

Clearly, there will always be a delay between these two steps. Problems arise when you are unable to meet your financial obligations because you are still waiting for payment.

When you are working on a project that is larger than usual, and you know there will be a substantial delay before you finally get paid, you will need to plan for that by ensuring you have a larger amount of working capital on hand to tide you over. By contrast, for smaller jobs where turnaround time is quite short, your working capital requirements will be minimal and your cash position will be relatively unaffected.

The real issues occur when delays are unexpected. For example, you may be doing a small renovation for a client and, while you have quoted the job and know how long it will take to complete, there is no way to be sure that the client will pay for it on time. Depending on the size of that job, you may wish to demand an upfront payment to cover the materials you need to pay for before commencing the job.

The key to successful cash management is carefully watching all the steps in the process and planning accordingly. The quicker you can make the cycle turn, the faster you can convert your trading operations back into cash, which means you will have increased liquidity in your business and will be less reliant on cash or extended trading terms from your suppliers.

Fortunately, you can manage your payments to suppliers, your work in progress and your debtors to improve your cash flow.

Managing payments to suppliers

While choosing the right supplier is paramount to your ability to provide a quality service and outcome for your client, many business owners don't realise that their choice of supplier will also affect their cash flow.

In some cases, you will be required to pay your suppliers upfront when you purchase materials, while others will allow you to purchase materials and supplies on credit. Both arrangements require different cash flow management strategies.

Here are some helpful hints to consider when choosing your supplier:

- Does your supplier provide the best quality product?

- Does your supplier have a returns policy?

- Does your supplier offer a competitive price?

- Do you use various suppliers for similar products? (It is important to have an alternate supplier for any given product to cover the risk that they cannot provide a product at any given time.)

- Does your supplier offer you credit terms?

- Does your supplier offer discounts for early or upfront payments?

Making full use of your payment terms with any supplier is effectively like having an interest-free loan. Therefore, it is important to manage your suppliers and the payments to them effectively.

For example, a client of mine is in property development and regularly goes to Bunnings to purchase a range of materials and tools for his developments. In the past, he would pay for all the items using his own credit card or cash, at an out-of-pocket cost of $5,000–$10,000 per month.

I asked him whether he had set up an account with Bunnings only to find, to my surprise, that he had not. Bunnings, like a number of suppliers, will offer trades an account and therefore credit terms. So we proceeded to set up an account online in a matter of minutes. It provides him a $10,000 credit limit with no fees and 60 days' interest-free terms. He even has the option to allocate job numbers to every purchase.

My client was able to free up his cash and his credit card and was able to save on interest he would otherwise have been charged. The additional hidden benefit was that he then had online statements, which slashed the amount of time he spent sorting out all the individual receipts and payments.

The real jewel in the above example is that he was able to use someone else's money (Bunnings) to purchase items that enabled him to continue to work on his developments to finish jobs and, ultimately, get paid. Unsurprisingly, his ability to manage his cash has increased greatly.

When you have established credit terms with a supplier, ensure you pay on the agreed terms, not early or late. And, where possible, seek to extend trading terms to assist with any fluctuations in cash flow.

In every relationship, communicate regularly and maintain a good working relationship with your suppliers so any future issues can be resolved with little or no impact to your business.

Managing work in progress

Work in progress is when you have been given an order for a job and you are in the process of working through it towards completion. Depending on the size of the job, this period can be quite lengthy and so you will need to manage the process well. After all, the sooner you complete the job, the earlier you can invoice and therefore get paid.

Here are some helpful hints to consider when managing work in progress:

- Record all the details of the job/order. You have a licensing requirement in building to provide the customer a written quote that stipulates all relevant details of the job. My recommendation would be to have a quote for every job you do, irrespective of size, to eliminate any potential confusion or miscommunication. Ensure you detail the specifics of the job, including:

  □ Start and finish dates (where possible)

  □ Any payments received

  □ Any progress payments to be made and timing of these payments

  □ Any additional requirements to be able to complete the job (for example, reliance on contractors or the client)

- Manage potential delays caused by the client by ensuring they are very clear on expectations of the job process and timing of payment or payments.

- Manage potential delays caused by contractors by ensuring they have booked your job in for the designated days/weeks and that they know whose responsibility it is to provide relevant materials and equipment.

- Manage potential delays caused by the work area in terms of location, access and power availability by planning for all those issues beforehand.

- Manage potential delays caused by external factors such as monitoring for bad weather or being aware of other public works in the area.

- Invoice immediately at all agreed points in time.

- Order materials and supplies when you are ready to commence, allowing for any lead times.

- Identify any potential bottlenecks, such as not having the right tradespeople on site at the right time, and look for alternatives, such as scheduling the job well and having others you can call on when needed.

- Ensure that you have the right levels of materials and supplies to complete the job, as delays in receiving goods will delay completion and therefore payment.

- Schedule all relevant labour to ensure they are ready and available when required, as other commitments could delay completion and therefore payment.

Managing debtors

Your sales income is the main cash flow driver of your business and converting that into cash is one of the most important processes in your business.

Clients who receive sales on credit are referred to as debtors. Managing payments due from debtors can consume both time and effort if proper controls and procedures are not in place from the outset.

Your customers are key to your business, however, until you receive payment for your services, effectively you have given them a donation, and you are not a charitable organisation.

Here are some helpful hints to consider when managing debtors:

- Establish payment terms and clearly communicate these at both quotation and invoice stage. You can also provide a reminder a couple of days prior to completing the job.

- Implement internal or external debt-collection systems to ensure all payment terms are met. Hire an internal debtor's clerk or use existing administration staff. Use an external service if your internal structure does not allow for it.

- Send out regular reminders and follow up on late payments.

- Meet regularly with your customers, particularly regular customers.

- Review payment terms for regular customers who continue to fall outside the agreed terms.

- When you become aware of a potential delay in a job, communicate with the customer and discuss alternatives, if possible.

- Only agree to a completion date with your customer when you are certain you can meet the deadline.

- Send out invoices as soon as work is complete, not at the end of the week or month.

- Send out invoices via email, not snail mail.

- Provide incentives to pay early, if appropriate.

- Offer alternative forms of payment, such as cash, cheque, credit card and EFT.

- Where commissions are payable, pay them on amounts when collected rather than on sale/invoice.

- Identify slow-paying customers and make contact early to discuss any issues.

- Monitor non-paying customers and keep in regular contact.

- Enter into payment arrangements for non-paying customers.

- Stop supply, if possible, for customers who have not met any agreed progress payments.

- Send letters of demand for long outstanding debts. If necessary, use a professional debt collector.

- Consider not performing any future jobs for customers who have been unreliable with payments.

Always remember that a good customer is one who pays. If you are not collecting payment from them, then your business is funding their business as well as your own.

MANAGING FINANCE

You can fund business operations and investment from debt (a loan from the bank or another third party), equity (your own funds), an equity partner (taking on an investor) or internal funds (profits).

Each of these options comes with its own set of risks and advantages, and it can sometimes be difficult to figure out the best option, or whether you should look for financing at all. Consequently, finance can be an extremely difficult and frustrating for business owners and, as such, needs to be planned for and executed as carefully and thoroughly as possible.

Let's consider the four types of financing, to help you determine which is right for you.

Debt	
Risks	**Advantages**
You may not be able to generate sufficient cash flow from your business operations to service the debt.	You retain control over your business by not having to answer to partners or investors.
You may be unable to repay the principle at the end of the loan period.	The profit and growth of the business is all yours as you would not have to share it with partners.
The level of security required for you to finance may leave your personal assets vulnerable if you cannot meet repayments.	Fixed repayments are agreed to from day one and you can better manage your cash flow.
You will need to pay interest on top of the sum borrowed, making the financing more expensive.	Lower cost of capital (interest payable) and raising debt finance (bank fees, insurance fees, legal/accounting fees).
You may be vulnerable to changes in interest rates.	Interest and associated costs are tax deductible.
If you are in the early stages of business, it can be difficult to get external finance.	

Personal equity	
Risks	**Advantages**
Putting your own money on the line means you bear the risk of the business and its ability to achieve the growth you require.	You can raise funds without exposing your personal assets to risk.
While it does not impose any significant cash flow requirements, it could take longer to generate the level of funding required.	You have no exposure to interest rates.
You might lose your capital if the business doesn't survive.	Less burden as there are no monthly loan repayments, improving cash flow.
No tax deductions are available as there are no servicing costs.	An improved financial profile with lenders and/or investors.
It can place strain on family relationships should personal financial obligations (such as meeting mortgage payments) be put under stress.	If you have prior credit issues, accessing debt could be a problem, whereas personal equity will bypass this hurdle.

An equity partner	
Risks	**Advantages**
You might lose control if they seek to acquire a share of your business.	You could benefit from mentoring support from the investor.
If you sell a share of the business, this could trigger a capital gains tax event.	Easier access to funds with less compliance requirements than banks.
Potential conflict with the investor.	No exposure to interest rates.
Greater pressure from the investor to achieve growth and higher returns.	External resources could add strategic input and alliances.
Need to establish an exit strategy.	A more stable financial structure.

Profit	
Risks	Advantages
Funds used from the business may impact negatively on business operations.	Increased profitability as there are no direct costs imposed on you and your business.
Reduced funds for working capital.	You have no exposure to interest rates.
Inability to cover unforeseen costs.	You retain control over the business.
	The growth of the business is all yours.
	Your assets are not vulnerable to creditors.

When it comes to choosing which financing option is right for you, there are a number of factors to consider.

If you are fortunate enough to have a profitable business and have maintained your cash reserves, using these funds can be one of the most favourable alternatives.

However, while the ideal scenario would be for all operations and investment to be funded by your profits, this may not always be possible due to cash flow requirements. Your ability to generate increased cash flow through good management of your working capital is very important. You need to be able to generate excess cash from your business operations to ensure this funding option is best suited to your circumstances. For this reason, you'll need to look at all possible alternate sources of funding to ensure you adopt the one most suitable to you and your business.

Getting the most out of debt finance

As long as your business can service the level of debt and has enough security to support the funding, debt finance can be a viable way to fund business operations. You will benefit by retaining ownership in respect of the growth and profitability of the business. Why give it away if you can afford not to?

There have been many businesses that have benefited from the use of debt financing as it has enabled them to grow, arguably, more than what they might have without it.

Consider one of my clients, who operates a business from an office warehouse that he used to lease for an annual rental amount of $66,000. The lease agreement had annual four per cent rent increases built in, which was a benefit to the landlord who was not only receiving more rent each year, but was also increasing the value of his property given commercial value is generally based on yield (or the percentage return on investment). In the first couple of years, it suited my client to rent given his personal circumstances, and the rent expense was fully tax deductible.

After a couple of years, he decided to buy the property he was renting as it suited his business requirements and had potential for some expansion. He successfully acquired the property for $1.35 million at a rate of 3.8 per cent, which meant his interest cost on the full loan amount was $51,300 per annum ($14,700 less than his rental payments). Beyond the annual cost savings, a secondary benefit was that he now had an asset that was increasing in capital value year on year.

As you can see, taking on the debt of the mortgage was a sensible business decision.

If you decide that debt financing is your best option then it is important to review a range of finance products from different lenders, as there are many options out there in today's market and you need to find the best option for your needs.

Not only are there various lenders, there are also various finance types, such as a bank overdraft, line of credit, credit card, cash flow lending, debtor finance, fully drawn advance, mortgage loan, interest only loan, lease and hire purchase and chattel mortgage, just to name a few.

The important thing here is to make sure you match the type of finance with the reason for the finance. That is, you want to match the term of the loan with the life of the asset you are funding.

Let's look at an example.

You need to upgrade the motor vehicle you use for your business, be it your ute, van or truck. Having made the decision to purchase the vehicle, the next decision is how you will pay for it. Let's assume paying it all up front is not an option, so you need to finance. Your options include a hire purchase agreement, a chattel mortgage, a line of credit or a personal loan.

Motor vehicles have an effective business life. In an ideal scenario, you would want to use that vehicle for a period of time where you are receiving the maximum benefit, both operationally and financially. Typically, that period is between three and seven years, depending on the type of vehicle, the kilometres you will drive and how it will be used (will you be carrying building materials in it or a regular basis or not?).

The most popular finance options for vehicles are hire purchase agreements and chattel mortgages. They are both taken out for a defined period of time (in years) and have the option of a balloon payment at the end of the period, meaning an amount you need to pay to buy it outright and pay back the finance. The balloon payment can be anywhere from zero to 50 per cent, depending on the length of the finance period and how the vehicle will be used. As a general rule, the shorter the period, the higher the balloon. The more the vehicle is driven, the lower the value of the vehicle and hence the lower the balloon.

The fundamental difference between a hire purchase and a chattel mortgage is that with the hire purchase you do not legally own the vehicle until the finance is paid out, whereas with the chattel mortgage you own the vehicle from day one. Other than that distinction, they both have very similar attributes from a financial perspective.

A line of credit, which is used solely for tax deductible business costs, could be a cheaper option as the interest rates are generally lower. If you have a line of credit already in place, it has the added advantage of no extra application process or fees. If the line of credit is not in the name of business, then you will need to apportion costs and allocate accordingly. For example, you may have a line of credit for an investment in another entity name, such as a trust, and the vehicle you are acquiring is for the business in the trading company. Therefore, you need to work out the amount of interest apportioned to the vehicle and account for that in the business company accounts so you get the full benefit of the tax deduction. This option is not ideal from the point of matching the finance to the asset and has the added complexity of one loan applying to various entities. While the line of credit is an option, from a trading business perspective it is generally used to manage working capital, not for motor vehicle purchases, as it is available on a long-term basis and generally secured against your property.

The other finance option for the vehicle is a personal loan. I would suggest this as a last resort due to the higher interest rates that are attached to such loans. It is very unlikely you would be in a position to have to use such a facility and I would not recommend it, other than in extreme circumstances.

In summary, this example shows that a hire purchase or chattel mortgage fits best, as its purpose is solely for the vehicle.

When dealing with banks and other lenders, you need to understand that they tend to be a little conservative regarding your business potential, especially when compared to your own thoughts. Of course, you know how well your business will perform with some additional funds; however, the banks need a little more persuasion and then there is that frustrating issue of red tape that they may force you to try and break through to get anything achieved.

What are banks looking for? Your bank wants to know as much about you and your business as possible so they can assess whether you are suitable for a loan. Some of the things the bank will want to see include:

- A description of your business, including and a brief history and where you are now.

- Your personal financial information, including personal assets and existing loans.

- Historical business financial information, including your profit and loss reports, balance sheets and tax returns (likely for a minimum of two years).

- Projected financial information, including cash flow forecasts and/or business plans.

- Details of what you require the loan for and why.

- If you have business partners, their personal information.

Providing all the above information in a complete and timely manner is the first step to showing the bank that you are well prepared and on top of your finances.

The bank will review this information to establish whether you will be able to support the loan with the required level of security, and service the loan with the required level of profits and cash flow. Therefore, the stronger your application, the more likely the bank will approve the loan. Keep in mind that your historical information is just that – historical – so you cannot do much there. Your cash flow forecast and business plan, on the other hand, are where you can really make a difference.

Finally, remember that numbers are just one aspect – don't forget the words that should go with them to demonstrate that you know exactly what is required and where you are headed. The level of confidence you have in your business and yourself will help increase the level of confidence the bank has in you and your business.

If you are faced with your loan application being denied, rather than getting angry, turn your energy towards finding out why. The better informed you are regarding this, the better prepared you will be to either seek alternative funding or review your strategy and prepare for when you are ready to make your next application.

Armed with this information, you could approach other lenders that may wish to deal with you, as their offering may be better aligned to your requirements.

You need to make sure you exhaust all options before giving up on the loan. I have had a number of clients who have not been successful on the first attempt, but then secured the loan they wanted from another lender. There are many lenders in the market and you should keep you options open. Start with the 'Big 4' banks and, if not successful, approach the second-tier financial institutions. There is an option is almost every situation.

Another alternative is to review your loan requirements and establish whether you may be able to reduce the funding amount required to achieve your goals. While this is not ideal, you may find that a lower funding amount may allow you to work towards your ultimate goal as servicing the loan is more manageable. Again, it will come down to your specific circumstances and requirements.

Assuming you do successfully get funding, you can be assured that your bank will require you to undergo reviews. At a minimum, this would be annually and, depending on the level of funding and your business situation, it could be as regularly as quarterly. Being well prepared for these reviews will show the bank that you understand their requirements and demonstrates that you have good internal management practices.

Keeping the lines of communication open with your banker will ensure they are ready to respond to any request you may have. The more you give, the more they do. If you do not provide information and respond to requests, then they will feel that there might be a problem with your business and will therefore become guarded and reserved in future dealings.

Refinancing

The other aspect of financing to be considered is refinancing an existing loan. It is always prudent to review your existing loans to make sure you are getting the best option available, especially since the cost of refinancing has dramatically reduced in recent years and lenders have become very competitive.

Some benefits of refinancing include:

- You could secure a lower interest rate, thereby reducing your repayments and improving your cash flow, or reducing the length of the loan.

- You could access increased finance for further investment, particularly if you have a good repayment history and your business has improved since the establishment of the original loan.

- Restructuring the type of loan may suit your future requirements. For instance, moving to a line of credit will provide you with access to money for future requirements without you having to apply for separate loans, which could be costly and time consuming.

- Consolidating existing debts will ease your cash flow and administrative requirements.

- Refinancing may allow you to release your personal assets as securities against existing loans.

Refinancing is simply about making sure you are in the best possible financial position with your lending, interest rates, servicing and access to future funds. There is no need to overcomplicate it, as we have discussed at length the options for managing your finance.

TROUBLESHOOTING

In this chapter, we've delved fairly deeply into financial management – so deep that you might be wondering whether all of this is necessary to achieve your goals. After all, it's just numbers.

I'm not so sure about that.

Financial management is all about having accurate, up-to-date financial information so you can make informed business decisions. You want to protect your investment and make sure that you don't do anything that can jeopardise that investment.

Good financial management will ensure that you can detect, if not prevent, any problems.

With this in mind, you'll need to make sure that your financial controls are detailed enough to provide you with enough information to make the right decisions.

Here is a list of some key controls:

- **Compare budgets and cash flows to results.** You need to ensure that budgets and cash flows are compared to actual results and that any significant variations are investigated and reviewed accordingly. Setting up the budgets and cash flow forecasts clearly define where your business is headed. Reviewing them regularly enables you to see how you are tracking so you can make any adjustments you need to get back on track.

- **Prepare financial information regularly.** Financial information should be prepared and available on a regular basis so you can make informed business decisions as required. With the advent of more sophisticated online accounting systems, you can get real-time data and reports on exactly where you are.

- **Approve all price and payment terms.** Ensure all sales quotes and orders are agreed and approved for price and payment terms. The better this is communicated to your customer the less likely problems will occur. It's one thing to get the job, it's another to get paid when you want/need to. Communicate regularly with your client.

- **Review debtors regularly for outstanding amounts.** In an ideal business world, you would have no debtors because every client would pay you on completion of the job. In the real world, this is not the case. So you need to make sure you are following up with clients to ensure they pay as soon as possible. Agree to suitable payment arrangements if need be.

- **Reconcile all bank accounts.** All accounts should be reconciled on a regular basis so you have accounted for all receipts and payments. That will allow you to know exactly where you sit with both your debtors and creditors and what your cash position is. In addition, it will provide accurate reporting so you're not missing anything and are therefore looking at up-to-date reports.

- **Ensure payments are approved and recorded.** All wages, salaries, commissions and contractor payments should be approved and accurately recorded. Your labour force is a major component of your costs for your business. You must check and review this cost regularly to make sure the correct payments are made and that any variation is investigated and accounted for. You need to make sure your employees' time is managed effectively and that your contractors are charging you for the work they have performed based on either quotes provided or your expectation of hours worked for the jobs completed.

- **Record all cash payments.** You need to ensure that any cash payments are recorded appropriately against accounting records. This may not sound important, but you may be surprised how much you and your business spends on its smaller expenses on a day-to-day basis. It could add up to be quite a significant amount by the end of the year, and you want to ensure that nothing is missed so you can claim your rightful tax deduction.

You need to put in place these controls to ensure that your business is protected.

A regular review of these procedures will ensure that you have good financial controls in your business so you can spend your time on growing your business and achieving your goals.

SUMMARY

We all want to make things easier and more efficient. In the building game, this has been made possible through innovation in tools, equipment processes and materials, all of which save you time, avoid problems and enable you to achieve more without extra effort. The same is true when it comes to money management – by adopting standard processes and systems in your business, you can save time, save money, solve problems and move towards the lifestyle you want.

CHAPTER 5: SUPPORT

'Give light and people will find the way.'
– Ella Baker

As a business owner in building and property development, there will be many times when it feels like you're on your own as you're managing the entire business. This industry has many demands and challenges, and you need to cover many bases.

One of the single biggest mistakes business owners make is that they try and do everything themselves. The reality is, you can't. At the very least, you shouldn't.

Financial management isn't your area of expertise. If it was, you'd be in accounting or financial planning, rather than building or property development. For you to personally manage your accounting and finances takes up far too much of your time and effort, which means it is taking time away from what you do best and, ultimately, costing your business money. Every hour you spend on accounting results in an hour lost on doing the things that actually generate dollars.

When you get out on site you know everything that needs to be done along with how and when it needs to be done. It's your job but, even more so, it's your life. It's who you are. There are, however, areas of business where you may not be as knowledgeable or efficient.

You can't be all things to all people, all of the time. The reality is that there are not enough hours in the day and there is not enough expertise in any individual to be able to achieve that.

So, what do you need?

Support.

You need the support of others to ensure that you don't leave a roof tile out of alignment or miss the final coat of paint in the ensuite.

Similarly, while you have the expertise to manage the operational functions well, you will need some assistance with the financial management of your business.

Why?

Because that's not where your expertise lies. Your knowledge and experience is in building and property development, not financial requirements and obligations. While you know the basics (in fact, more than the basics after reading this book!), there is always more to learn when it comes to making your business as successful as it can be. For this reason, you need to have the right people supporting you that do.

Who can help?

Your own personal chief financial officer (CFO).

A CFO is the most senior executive of a business who is responsible for its financial control and planning. They are in charge of all of the accounting functions of the business, including preparing financial statements and budgets, credit control, monitoring expenditure, managing cash flow, coordinating finance and capital raising, managing investment, managing all taxation and other compliance requirements, and reporting financial performance and financial data to the chief executive officer (CEO).

You are the CEO.

A CEO is the most senior executive of a business who is responsible for the overall operational management and performance of the business. They are in charge of the strategic direction of the business. They are ultimately responsible for operations, sales and marketing, human resources and finance. They make all the key decisions in the business in all those areas. The smaller the business, the more hands-on they are.

In your business, you are the CEO because you are the person who is in control of operations. You are the builder and/or property developer with your skills focused in that area. Generally speaking, sales and finance are areas where you do not have the same level of training and experience, however, they are areas that are critical to your business success.

You typically cover the sales area by advertising, whether that is online or in traditional print, by setting up a website and, in today's world, via social media. You may also be connected to network groups, local communities, sporting clubs and more, and you will generate sales via referrals from former customers.

When it comes to finances, the CEO has oversight of the business's financial decisions and makes decisions around key investments. However, the CFO is the one who does the bulk of the management.

What do you do if you don't have a CFO? Employ one?

Not all businesses can afford the luxury of employing a full-time CFO, particularly, small- to medium-sized businesses. So, what then?

The answer is simple. You employ a virtual CFO.

Now I hear you ask, 'What is a virtual CFO?'

A virtual CFO is essentially the same as a CFO, but fills the role on a part-time basis for a fraction of the cost of a full-time CFO.

The virtual CFO is your personal financial adviser – someone who becomes the trusted source for financial perspective. Someone you can trust who works closely with you and your business to help you make the right decisions to improve the financial management of your business, and your business's performance as a result. They act as a sounding board and provide financial sanity to you and your business. In these tough economic times, a virtual CFO will provide you with the valuable insight you need to navigate your way to success.

Your virtual CFO will enable you to take advantage of a level of expertise not previously available to you, which will now enable you to run your operation while knowing that all your financial matters are being taken care of by a highly qualified and experienced adviser.

Outsourcing this part of your business makes perfect sense. If you have a plumbing issue, you hire a plumber. If you need an electrician, you get one. If you want to get fit, you engage a personal trainer. If you want a financially healthy business, you get yourself a virtual CFO.

Doing so will resolve your financial management issues.

You will no longer have to base all your financial business decisions on gut feel. Instead, you will have sound, informed financial advice at your fingertips.

You will no longer have to worry about what the numbers mean in all those financial reports and tax returns. You will have them explained clearly so you understand what they all mean and why they are important.

You will no longer feel like your efforts are not being rewarded financially.

You will have the required expertise alongside you to convert your effort into dollars.

If you do it, you will never look back.

WORKING WITH A VIRTUAL CFO VERSUS DOING IT YOURSELF

When should you work with a virtual CFO, rather than doing everything yourself?

If you are an ambitious business owner who wants to truly grow your business in the most efficient way possible, then the simple answer is always.

However, the commercially realistic answer is that it's time to engage a virtual CFO when you are spending so much time on the financial management of your business that it is taking you away from profit-generating activities, or the sales and operations of your business.

In the early stages of your business, you will have the time to manage the basic financial aspects because you may not be fully occupied every day with actually performing jobs. As your business grows, it might become difficult for you to continue to handle the financial management as you look to grow your business to the next phase. One of the first signs that it is time to consider a virtual CFO is when your attention moves away from financial management. If you have taken on all the bookkeeping for your business, paying employees, contractors and suppliers, receipting payments and managing your cash flow, those responsibilities can fall to the wayside when you get a project or job that seems more important and requires your full attention.

At this point, you know that your business needs to take the next step towards growth, and a virtual CFO is required to help you plan for this growth.

You will also need your virtual CFO for your financing requirements, particularly as your business grows. They will help decide if financing is appropriate and, if so, what type of finance will best suit your business and then prepare you sufficiently for the finance application process to provide the best possible chance for approval.

Even if you have systems in place for your financial accounts, your virtual CFO is able to work with your bookkeeper and finance officer to identify and measure exactly what is driving your business performance and where you should be focusing. Conversely, they will identify what it is that could be causing you problems.

If you have issues with your cash flow, you will generally know that, however, you may not know exactly why or how to resolve those issues. There are many reasons for cash flow problems and some of those you may not even be considering, such as sudden growth or winning a large new client or contract. These things are great, but only if they are managed well financially because they could turn very bad, very quickly. Worse case, you could lose that new client or contract because you cannot manage it well and provide the level of service required.

If your financial reports are not making sense or you do not believe they are correct, you may need some help from an experienced financial adviser. Your virtual CFO will make sure the financial reports are accurate and they will then make sure you understand them and what they mean to your business. Together you will work through them to monitor your business performance and put in place the measures to improve those areas that need attention.

You will know when you are not managing the financial part of your business efficiently enough to help you with your business. All you need to do is be honest with yourself and make the decision to look for that support.

WHAT ARE THE DIFFERENT WAYS A VIRTUAL CFO CAN HELP YOU AND YOUR BUSINESS?

You can work with a virtual CFO in a couple of different ways. How you do so will depend on the level of support you require.

You are able to use the services of a virtual CFO as little or as much as you would like, although the true essence of working with a virtual CFO is an ongoing arrangement so you receive the maximum benefit for you and your business.

The typical working arrangement with a virtual CFO is ongoing monthly or quarterly guidance and advice, including the following services:

- Bookkeeping

- Accounting

- Income tax returns

- Activity statements

- ASIC compliance

- Strategic planning and advice

- Budgeting

- Cash flow management

- Performance management and financial reporting

- Tax planning

The alternative arrangement is to use your virtual CFO on a specific project basis, which could include services such as:

- Strategic planning

- Business plans

- Budgeting

- Cash flow forecasting,

- Development of key performance indictors (KPIs)

- Profitability analysis and improvements

- Cash strategies

- Financing or capital raising

- Systems assessment and development

- Due diligence

- Business valuations

- Mergers and acquisitions

- Exit strategies

The reality is that you can tailor the virtual CFO services to suit your specific needs. Your virtual CFO will take the time to understand your unique challenges and needs, and will help you develop a tailored solution to achieve your goals faster and more efficiently.

One of the benefits of having a virtual CFO is that they are flexible and can adapt to your changing needs. As your business grows, so does their level of service and support because you are not just working with a single professional, you have a team of professionals behind you.

HOW DO YOU CHOOSE A VIRTUAL CFO?

Listed below are the most important attributes you should seek in a virtual CFO:

- **Qualification:** They must be qualified to a minimum level of Certified Practicing Accountant (CPA) or Chartered Accountant (CA). This will confirm that they are educated to a superior level, as these organisations not only require the tertiary qualifications, but they also require postgraduate studies and continued professional development for every year they run their practice. This will provide you with a technically skilled and educated team of professionals to work with you.

- **Experience:** They must be able to display that they have at least ten years of experience working with businesses on all facets of tax compliance, financial reporting and analysis, strategic planning, cash flow management, financing and advisory services. In addition, the more experience they have in your industry, the better service they will be able to provide.

- **Communication:** They must be good communicators and be able to clearly explain and demonstrate the advice they provide so you are able to clearly understand that advice. They should not only be able to work well with yourself, as the business owner, but also with all your key employees that they are likely to liaise with over the life of the relationship.

- **Analysis:** They must be analytical in nature. Any accountant who has the relevant qualification and experience is able to prepare annual tax returns. CFOs, however, are much more. Not only are they able to prepare all of your compliance requirements, they are able to review and assess the financial position of your business and provide feedback on which areas need attention. Having done that, they will then offer different solutions.

- **Strategy:** They must be strategic thinkers, always looking towards the future and to you achieving your goals. Your virtual CFO should be able to work with you to develop strategies that suit your long-term vision and then help you deliver those strategies. Having delivered those strategies, they need to be flexible and adaptable to be able to cope with changing competitive dynamics, differing customer needs, new technologies and the ever-changing regulatory environment.

- **Risk:** They must be very mindful of all the exposures to risk in your business. Risk is rapidly becoming one of the most important factors in business and, with continued regulatory changes and restrictions, it must be front of mind at all times in every facet of your business. The ability to make your business resilient and strengthen your structure and processes is a key trait to look for in a virtual CFO.

- **Technology:** They must be up-to-date with all relevant technology that can assist you in the financial management of your business. Technology continues to evolve and you want your virtual CFO to be able to evolve with it. This will not only create efficiencies in your business, it will also provide opportunities to innovate.

- **Passion:** They need to care about you and your business and your continued growth. This will ensure they do everything in their power to help you reach your goals.

Before deciding on your virtual CFO, you should do a little research on them. What you should be looking for is whether they meet the criteria listed previously. Some of those attributes can be easily determined, such as their qualifications and experience. However, the remaining attributes will require meeting with them.

Think of the first meeting with your virtual CFO as an interview – this is someone you will be working closely with and, hopefully, for some time. Just some of the questions you could ask include:

- I see your firm is (CPA or CA). Are all your accountants qualified accordingly? (Remember, you might find yourself working with different members of the team.)

- You appear to have the experience in years but have you worked with many businesses in building and property development?

- Can you give me some examples of the type of clients you currently working with that would be similar to me?

- Can you give some examples of how you've helped similar businesses with their tax compliance?

- How have you helped similar business owners protect their personal and business assets? Can you give me an example?

- What strategies have you used to help your clients improve their cash flow?

- Do you use and/or do you clients use the latest technology in their business? If so, did you recommend and/or implement the systems? How has it helped them?

- Have you not been able to help a business owner better manage his finances? If so, why? What was the outcome?

- Some of my strategic goals are (explain some of the goals you'd like to achieve in the next one to three years). What are some ways we could go about achieving them?

Depending on your level of comfort, you may wish to ask more questions and be even more specific about how this virtual CFO can help you. That's totally fine because you need to be sure.

Having gone through this process, the only attributes that you didn't ask about are the ones that will answer themselves, being communication and passion.

It's now up to you.

CONCLUSION

'It always seems impossible until it's done.'
– Nelson Mandela

Give yourself a clap. Seriously – you deserve it.

Together we have covered many areas to help you understand all the financial aspects you need to consider to grow your business into a financially rewarding, tax-efficient, lifestyle business.

You've learnt to create a strategic plan, defining where you are now, where you want to go and how to navigate the road between the two.

You've learnt the key considerations when it comes to choosing the most appropriate structure for your business, which will protect your personal assets, help you find funding when you need it, reduce tax, keep costs and administration down, and plan for the future.

You've discovered your statutory requirements and how you can stay on the right side of the ATO and the various other agencies that regulate the business landscape.

You've delved deep into managing your money – your day-to-day cash flow, getting finance and troubleshooting for the future.

And you've learnt how to find the support you need to integrate all of this new knowledge into your business.

It's now in your hands. Having just established all the things you need to not only consider, but implement, for the effective financial management of your business, it is now decision time.

What will you do?

You have two options.

The first is to do nothing and keep things the way they are, irrespective of whether you're happy with your current situation.

The second option is to take action.

You may know what you would like to achieve, but just ask yourself, 'Do I know how to get there from where I am now?'

You may think that your structure is sound, just like the concrete slab you have laid on your current building project, but just ask yourself, 'Would it hurt me to have that reviewed and confirmed to make sure that it best suits my particular circumstances?'

You may think that you are meeting all your compliance requirements and satisfying all the relevant authorities, such as the ATO, ASIC, SRO, Land Titles Office, WorkCover Authority, your superannuation provider and even your bank. However, just ask yourself, 'Am I really meeting all these requirements and am I dealing with them in the most efficient way possible?'

You may think that you have an efficient money management system in place, but just ask yourself, 'Am I making the most of what I have available, leveraging finance to grow my business and troubleshooting for the future?'

You might think you have the right support structures in place, or even that you can do it all yourself, but just ask yourself, 'Is managing my own accounting and bookkeeping the best use of my time when I could be taking advantage of new business opportunities?'

It's time to get those questions answered and to find out whether your business is really positioned to help you create the lifestyle you want. If it is, fantastic! If it isn't, then you can take action *now* to set yourself on the path to success.

I understand that you may not want to confront the fact that you might not be doing things the way you should be (if at all), but please don't worry about that. If you think that way, it will stifle your ability to do anything or get anywhere, let alone where you actually want to go.

Instead, what you should be concerned about is not being able to live the life you want and create the success you deserve, because what isn't working now is going to continue to cause you pain. I know you don't want that and I certainly don't want that for you.

The time for thinking is over. Now it's time to *do*.

APPENDICES

APPENDIX A:
TAXATION ISSUES FOR PROPERTY DEVELOPMENTS

There are many tax and legal issues when dealing in the property development space.

It can be a potential minefield.

Fortunately, by understanding the lay of the land you will be in a much better position to protect yourself, or to ask your accountant or financial adviser the right questions to prevent you from being caught out by the ATO.

The key issue for property developments is the distinction between *capital* and *revenue*.

Why?

Put simply, there are different tax treatments for each revenue type, and any profits or gains that can be considered capital can receive significant tax concessions as opposed to those that are considered to be revenue.

The tax consequences arising from any property development fall into three categories:

1. The mere realisation of a capital asset.

2. An isolated profit-making transaction or scheme.

3. Income from carrying on a business.

Tax on mere realisation of a capital asset

A capital asset is something that you acquire with the intention of holding it and generating a return from it and not for the purpose of profit-making by sale. For example, a residential or commercial property that you hold for a period and rent would be considered a capital asset, irrespective of whether you renovate it or not. A capital asset would also extend to land that you purchase and then develop and rent when complete. You can see that the definition centres around the 'hold' strategy, rather than selling in the short-term.

A 'mere realisation' refers to the gain you make from a capital asset. If you eventually decide to sell the property that you purchased, held and rented for a period of time (as described above), and there was a profit due to a natural increase in value, this would be considered to be a mere realisation.

If, on the other hand, you bought a property with the intention of renovating it and selling it for a profit, that would be considered to be a profit-making transaction or scheme (which I'll cover shortly).

A mere realisation will be on the capital account, so you could access capital gains tax (CGT) concessions as a result.

CGT applies to any asset acquired after 20 September 1985, unless specifically excluded, such as your family home, car and other personal assets. Assets depreciated in a business are also excluded from CGT as they are counted against your revenue. As an Australian resident, CGT applies to all assets owned anywhere in the world. As a foreign resident, CGT applies to all taxable Australian property.

While you may be subject to CGT as opposed to income tax for any profits or gains made in a property development, you may be eligible for tax concessions.

For instance, if the asset was held in the name of an individual, trust or superannuation fund for more than 12 months, you are entitled to a CGT discount – 50 per cent for individuals and trusts and 33.33 per cent for superannuation funds. Therefore, you can potentially half your profit or gain if the asset is held in the right entity.

In other words, if you were to make a capital gain of $200,000 and you held the asset in your individual name or in a trust, you would be eligible for a 50 per cent CGT discount. Therefore, you would declare $100,000 as net income in your tax return and pay tax at your marginal rate (individual) or the marginal rates of the respective beneficiaries (trust). The highest rate of tax you would pay is currently 49 per cent inclusive of Medicare levy, or a total of $49,000.

How do you know if your sale is going to be considered on capital account?

The courts place a significant emphasis on your intention at the time you purchase an asset and whether your intention is to sell the asset for a profit, or whether your intention was to hold the asset for a longer-term purpose. As mentioned earlier, if an asset held for a longer-term purpose was then sold, the profit would be due to natural increase in value.

An example of the mere realisation of a capital asset is as follows:

Mr Pipe operated his plumbing business as a sole trader. With some savings for a deposit and available equity in his own home, he decided to purchase a residential property as an investment and rented the property for three years. Mr Pipe then sold the property at a large profit when property values had greatly increased. Mr Pipe's profit is not income because the purchase and eventual sale of the residential property, in this scenario, is not considered a business operation. It was the purchase and sale of an investment, irrespective of whether he had a significant purpose of profit-making in the long-term.

Tax on profit-making transactions

Unlike a mere realisation of an asset's value, a profit-making transaction is one where an asset was purchased with the intent of selling it for profit. This transaction is considered revenue, rather than capital (even if it's an isolated or one-off transaction), which means that the net profit from the transaction will be included in the tax return of the entity that holds the asset.

In other words, if you were to make a profit of $200,000 and you held the asset in your individual name or a trust, you would declare the full $200,000 as net income in your tax return and pay tax at your marginal rate (individual) or the marginal rates of the respective beneficiaries (trust). The highest rate of tax you would pay is currently 49 per cent (inclusive of Medicare levy) or $98,000. If the entity was a company, you would pay 30 per cent of the profit in tax ($60,000) or 28.5 per cent ($57,000), depending on whether your company qualifies as a small business entity with turnover of $2 million or less.

As mentioned earlier, the key distinction between a mere realisation and a profit-making transaction is your intention when you purchase the asset.

There have been many cases that have been before the courts on this issue of capital vs revenue and whether property was purchased with the intention to sell for a profit or hold for rental purposes.

In what may seem an extreme case, a property developer had held a parcel of land for 20 years and due to her history and the fact that the land was 'ripe for subdivision' and she was aware of this, it was held that the land was purchased for resale at a profit.

In other cases, townhouses were developed and never offered for rent and as such were considered to be developed for the purpose of sale at a profit.

An example of a property sale considered to be on revenue account is as follows:

Mr Veritas purchased a property as his primary residence and lived in that property for a few years. He then subdivided and developed the property with two units at the rear of the property. At completion, the properties were listed with a real estate agent for sale. The properties were success-fully sold shortly after completion.

The profits derived from the development and sale of properties that were not offered or held for rent are income. In determining whether there is a purpose of profit-making, the actions of Mr Veritas in subdividing and developing the property to make profits from the sale of property indicate that the purpose was profit-making. The sale of the properties was consid-ered to be on revenue account and assessed accordingly.

Tax on income-generating businesses

When would you be considered to be operating a business of property development?

Your property development is considered to be a business where you have a history of property development. If you are considering investing in your first property development, that is most likely to be considered a mere realisation or a profit-making transaction, as discussed earlier. However, if you are planning your third or fourth development, it is more likely to be seen as a regular business activity. As a result, you will be required to account for transactions relating to your property development on the revenue account.

In these circumstances, the land involved in these business transactions will be considered trading stock, not unlike coffee supplies for a café or clothing for a clothing retailer. For example, the café business sold $100,000 in coffee to its customers and the cost of the coffee for those sales was $25,000. The $25,000 of cost is a deductible expense. The same applies to land. If you sold land for $500,000 and the cost of that land was $400,000, the cost is deductible as an expense of trading stock in the financial year that the sale takes place.

So how can you know whether an isolated transaction would be considered a business operation or commercial transaction for a profit-making purpose? The ATO will consider the following factors:

(a) The nature of the entity undertaking the operation or transaction.

(b) The nature and scale of other activities undertaken by the taxpayer.

(c) The amount of money involved in the operation or transaction and the magnitude of the profit sought or obtained.

(d) The nature, scale and complexity of the operation or transaction.

(e) The manner in which the operation or transaction was entered into or carried out.

(f) The nature of any connection between the relevant taxpayer and any other party to the operation or transaction.

(g) If the transaction involves the acquisition and disposal of property, the nature of that property.

(h) The timing of the transaction or the various steps in the transaction.

What does this mean for you and your property development?

If the ATO considers you to be conducting a business of property development, then your profit from such activities will be taxed on the revenue account, in the same way as profit-making transactions (as explained earlier). Your profit will be included in the tax return of the entity that is conducting the business and taxed accordingly. No access would be available to any CGT concessions.

When your property development changes

The basic tax position for a property development is:

- A capital asset is something that you acquire with the intention of holding it and generating a return from it.

- Activities you undertake in respect to the property may amount to the carrying on of a business, or an isolated profit-making transaction.

- If you dispose of a capital asset, then CGT provisions apply.

- Merely claiming a capital intention may not be sufficient to meeting the approval of the ATO or the courts.

- If you enhance the value of a capital asset in order to increase the return when it is sold (for example: you obtain development approval for a farm) you may still be 'merely realising' the capital asset, or maybe not, depending on the degree of enhancement and all the factors considered in farm cases.

- If your activities with a capital asset become more than mere realisation (or an initial capital intention cannot be established), you cannot access CGT concessions and you will then need to consider the income tax consequences.

- Your intention in relation to a capital asset can change.

The final point here is key – your intention in relation to a capital asset can change.

A capital asset may turn into a profit-making transaction or business. The land may not have been originally purchased with a profit-making intention, however, due to changing circumstances, it may then venture into a business or profit-making transaction.

Let's explore this issue with an example.

Mr Beach purchased ten acres of land in 2002 in a fairly remote seaside location so he and his family could enjoy the benefits of holidaying at the beach. In 2010, following discussions with friends and colleagues, some of which had experience in property development, he decided to subdivide and develop the land. The predominate reason was the significant increase in land value at this now rather popular seaside location. As a secondary issue, the family were no longer using the land for their recreation as they once were. Mr Beach embarked on a significant development with 50 residential lots. The subdivided land was then sold at a significant profit.

In this scenario, the profit on the development would be considered on revenue account. Once Mr Beach decided to develop due to the significant increase in land value and the interest in property in the area, the land transformed from one which was held for 'domestic purposes' for the owner to one that was purely driven to engage in a commercial venture to make a profit. The transformation turned the development from a 'mere realisation' to an assessable transaction. Mr Beach had 'ventured into' a profit-making scheme and the land was no longer held on capital account.

While this particular scenario may be rare, the fact remains that the ATO and the courts will closely examine the facts of any scenario and will look to clarify whether the intention and/or purpose has changed from one that would be considered capital to a business or profit-making scheme and therefore on revenue account.

There have been many legal cases in this area, particularly ones involving farmers looking to undertake subdivision activities themselves, rather than simply offloading the farm to a property developer.

The theme that developed from these farming cases was that if the farmer didn't look too much like they were actively doing things a developer would do, the transactions would be considered a mere realisation of a capital asset to maximise the return to the farmer on the disposal of the family farm. If there is a rule of thumb, it is that the greater the direct involvement of the farmer in the subdivision activities, the more likely they would have stepped over the line into the business of property development, where the profits are then subject to tax on revenue account.

Similarly, in the example above with Mr Beach, if he simply decided to seek a subdivision and sell without any development, it may well have been considered a mere realisation of a capital asset.

The law in this area is not just about mere realisations becoming development activities, or how long an asset has been held; it also looks at profit-making intention and isolated profit-making transactions amounting to something less than a business.

Without wanting to generalise, the test with isolated profit-making transactions or one-off ventures is whether you intend to make a profit from entering into the transaction.

There have been many cases that have looked closely at this issue of intention and purpose. What they tell us is that you must prove you didn't have a profit-making intention in order for the transactions to be taxed as a capital gain.

In a perfect world, you, as the property developer, will get tax advice when you are considering any developments and ensure that there is documentary evidence of your intention at the appropriate time. (Hopefully you're reading this book before your first development!)

In the real world, though, there are often conflicts between your stated intentions and the activities you actually undertake, including documents and plans provided to financiers and others.

While the ATO talks about wrongful and inappropriate claims and exploitation of the system, litigation about the distinction between capital and revenue has been happening ever since there were different tax outcomes depending on how profits were categorised, and there is no one size fits all tax treatment for property development.

There will always be commercial activities that start out as capital, and which require a change of plans for a host of reasons, including liquidity and changed market conditions. Such a change is not, on its own, a problem from a tax point of view.

At the end of the day it all boils down to the facts and circumstances of each particular case, and how much appetite you have for engaging in potentially lengthy and costly disputes with the ATO.

The ATO is willing to take on clever arguments about developments on capital account. However, it may not be the clever argument that lets you down, it's all about the stuff that lawyers always get excited about, evidence. Consequently, you must document your intentions at the time of acquisition and monitor changes of use while you hold the development.

SUMMARY

Tax law can be confusing for new property developers, as it can be a challenge to determine in which category your development should fall, as well as what should happen if you change your strategy (moving from selling a property to renting it out, for instance). Here professional advice is key to ensure you properly take advantage of any concessions while avoiding any pitfalls.

APPENDIX B:
STRUCTURING YOUR PROPERTY DEVELOPMENT

If you are considering getting into property development, you could structure the development as a sole trader, partnership, company or trust. As with
your main business, many developers will protect themselves by using a
separate entity (a company or trust) for each development.

However, the ownership of the land on which the development is to occur
often determines the development entity, so it is important to get this right
so you don't run the risk of paying additional stamp duty by having to
transfer ownership.

Whatever entity and development arrangement you adopt, it is vital that
you clearly identify and document the identity and role played by each
party.

Beyond the structures covered earlier in this book, there are some additional legal structures common in the property development space that
are worth considering – special purpose vehicles, joint ventures and self-
managed superannuation funds.

Special purpose vehicles

A special purpose vehicle (SPV) is a separate formal structure (either a company or a trust) that brings together separate parties, such as a developer and an investor, for the purpose of a property development.

These property developments usually exist for a defined time period and are generally born from the developer having the idea for a project and the investor, liking the idea, investing in the project. At the completion of the project, each party then goes their own way.

SPVs can be a beneficial structure when you would like the return from a development to be classified as the realisation of a capital asset, rather than a revenue-generating activity. However, in order to access the CGT concessions, the SPV would need to be in a trust structure, as companies cannot access the CGT concessions.

The reason for this is that an SPV would be legally separate from any other revenue-generating property development activities being carried on. Therefore, it could be argued that the new SPV is a clean slate, unaffected by previous property developments and demonstrating the intention to realise a capital asset from day one.

If external factors cause you to sell the development much earlier than the build-and-hold strategy anticipated then, unless the ATO can prove otherwise, the initial capital intention may still hold up, even if the property has only been held for a relatively short period of time (remembering that you would need to hold the asset for a period of 12 months to access the 50 per cent CGT discount).

The factors that the ATO would look to investigate in order to prove a revenue-generating development, rather than one on capital account are:

The parties have experience in property development, selling property and construction and the underlying purpose may be for development and sale.

- Finance documents for the development may indicate the dwellings, once complete, will be sold within a certain time period in order to repay part or all of the loan.

- Communication with local authorities granting building approvals may describe the activity as being a development of property for sale.

- Real estate agents may be engaged early in the development process, along with advertising being undertaken.

- The property/s are sold very soon after the 12-month CGT concession period.

All the above factors may provide the ATO with enough evidence to suggest that the intention from the outset of the development was a profit-making venture or scheme, and therefore taxable on revenue account with no access to the 50 per cent CGT concession.

However, keep in mind that this is a complex area and should be discussed with your accountant or financial adviser. The ATO has made clear its intention to audit developers to determine if they are accounting for their transactions in accordance with tax law, with penalties of up to 75 per cent of the tax avoided, in addition to the requirement to pay the avoided tax, for deliberate avoidance cases.

In these cases, the ATO is saying that the correct tax treatment is to tax profits as revenue and not as capital, and that an SPV arrangement is a contrived attempt to use trusts (in particular) as vehicles to access the CGT discount.

In other words, the ATO may believe that the trust is set up to try and isolate what might otherwise be a natural part of the other commercial property transactions you undertake.

The ATO may also believe that you justify capital account treatment on the strength of your claimed intentions to build and hold for income-generation purposes, and that subsequent transactions that appear more consistent with build and sell strategies are explained as being driven by changed circumstances.

The commercial reality is that there will be activities that start out as being capital in nature and then require a change for various reasons. These could be due to cash flow issues or changed market conditions. The change itself is not necessarily the problem if there is a genuine commercial explanation which has contributed to it.

In any case, if you set out your intention in SPV documents, it is likely to be a good starting point. Be as prepared as you possibly can.

Joint venture arrangements

Property development arrangements have been on the ATO's radar for a very long time and we are currently seeing audit activity looking at the GST treatment of joint venture (JV) arrangements.

One of the problems with understanding JVs is that the term itself is used in a number of different ways. Let's explore that.

An Incorporated JV can simply be an arrangement between parties that they will undertake a commercial activity through a company which may own the relevant property. So you could have two or more shareholders in that company.

An Unincorporated JV is a different beast – it is a contractual arrangement between two or more parties to undertake a particular commercial activity and commonly involves some parties contributing property (or the use of property) which they remain the owners of.

A common question that comes up at this point is, if a JV is an arrangement between two or more parties, how is it different to a partnership?

A partnership is where two or more people are in business together with a view to sharing profit. Tax law states that two or more people in receipt of income jointly will constitute a partnership for tax purposes. A common example of a partnership for tax purposes is where two or more people jointly hold a rental property. They are in receipt of rental income jointly from the property they own and therefore they constitute a partnership for tax purposes.

In a JV, on the other hand, the participants don't share profits – they each have an entitlement to the output of the undertaking. For example, a land owner might contribute vacant land to a joint venture together with preliminary work performed to seek approval for a development, while a builder then obtains further approvals and builds properties on the land. The finished properties are then distributed equally to each of the participants of the JV to do with as they wish. They might choose to live in the completed properties, rent them or sell them.

From a tax perspective, each participant accounts for their tax treatment separately, given that the (unincorporated) JV is not a separate taxpayer. In other words, there are two or more separate entities, not one combined entity (like a company) with shareholders.

JVs can also simplify the way they account for GST externally and internally where revenue is connected to the JV activity by establishing a GST JV. According to the ATO's GST regulations, GST JV purposes include 'the design, or building, or maintenance of residential or commercial premises'. This does not include land subdivision.

JVs, if structured correctly, have a number of benefits over other structures, such as partnerships. The parties in a JV can adopt their own tax treatment for their participation in a JV and they are not jointly and severally liable (I'll cover this in more detail shortly). If the JV is structured so that there is no need to transfer property, duty and tax costs may be avoided or deferred.

The possibility of CGT, stamp duty and other tax costs at the completion of the project needs to be carefully considered. As a general rule, if you are dealing with real property and accept that a true JV requires a sharing of output, rather than profit, this may require a change in ownership interests in the property that can trigger tax costs. The structure and documentation of a JV of this type will likely determine the timing of these costs.

For instance, because transferring land will trigger stamp duty to the buyer and CGT to the seller, it may be beneficial to trigger the transfer at the beginning of the project where the value of land may be at its lowest point to minimise both stamp duty and CGT. Conversely, it may work as well at the end of the project once all development costs have been factored into the project. The key here is to plan the project carefully and in detail from the outset so you can make any land transfers necessary at the most advantageous time of the development.

The income tax treatment of the JV by the parties will depend on the actual arrangements entered into and the extent of the property development being undertaken.

Getting it wrong

The benefits of an unincorporated JV include that there is no joint and several liability. In other words, each of the parties in the joint venture is responsible for their own tax consequences and one cannot impinge on the other. The real-life problems that arise if you have created an accidental partnership are shown in the following example.

Consider two friends, Mark and Brian, who formed a JV for their property development, making a point of documenting that the arrangement was not a partnership in their initial agreement.

To obtain finance to complete the project, Brian needed to put up his family home as collateral. Because of this, Mark and Brian formed a new agreement, which contained the following clause:

'The parties have agreed that, notwithstanding their co-registered proprietor shares of the property, they will have equal shares in the property as tenants-in-common and will share equally all costs, liabilities, mortgages and proceeds derived from any sale arising from the property.'

So Mark and Brian agreed that they would have equal shares in the property, that they would share all costs equally, and that they would share all proceeds (or profits) equally. As discussed earlier, one of the defining features of a partnership is that the partners receive an equal share of the profits, while in a JV each party is entitled to an output of the undertaking. Consequently, this new clause meant Mark and Brian were now considered to be a tax partnership, even though it may not have been their intention.

Upon completion of the development, the properties were sold and the GST liability, as issued by the ATO, was $508,962. Brian paid his share of the GST liability ($254,481), believing that the Mark would also pay his share. Unfortunately, Mark did not. The ATO then pursued Brian for the Mark's share on the basis that they were a partnership (I think you know where this is going).

The ATO was successful and Brian was liable for the full GST liability – $508,962.

The key issue for consideration was whether there was in fact a JV in place. It was concluded that while the first agreement was a JV, the subsequent agreement changed the entitlements from sharing the properties developed (a feature of a JV) to a share of 'joint or collective' profits (a feature of a partnership).

Consequently, Brian, as a partner in the partnership created by the subsequent agreement, was jointly and severally liable for the full amount of the GST owing. If it was found that there was a genuine JV in place, he would have only been liable for his half of the GST liability.

As you can see, care needs to be taken in any JV development.

JVs in other structures

What if you decided to use a company or unit trust as the JV vehicle?

The key difference between the partnership JV and company or unit trust from a structuring point of view is the issue of losses. In a partnership JV, the losses on a current year basis are able to be claimed by each of the parties in their respective entities and can therefore help to offset other income and potentially reduce their tax liability. When it comes to a company and/ or unit trust structure, unfortunately, the losses are quarantined against future profits and as such you are unable to offset these losses on a current year basis against other income you may be generating.

Entering into a development agreement or construction contract between the entity developing the land (building company) and the entity holding the land (land owner) is one alternative that would allow the building to take up the costs of the development as they are incurred on a year-by-year basis.

Development agreements

A development agreement is a contractual arrangement between the builder and land owner for which there is a fee for the development of the land.

This arrangement differs from a typical JV where the result is a sharing of the final product (the completed houses, units or apartments), as the development arrangement will be a sharing of the profits by the land owner paying the builder a fee for the development of the land.

These agreements are best structured as to equalise the profits as best is possible.

The two main types of agreements are to either:

1. Structure a development agreement for a fee for costs plus a percentage of profit on sale of the units.

2. Structure a fixed fee that has a contingency based on the success of the project. In other words, the fee could be reduced if the expected return was not achieved.

These agreements have the benefit of eliminating any stamp duty that would be paid by transferring the ownership of the land from the original land owner to the newly created entity that would run the development (a significant cost, depending on the value of the original land used in the development).

Self-managed super funds

From a tax perspective, your self-managed superannuation fund (SMSF) is a good place to make property development profits, provided you won't need to access the money until retirement.

The downside is that it also involves cutting a path through a jungle of complex tax and legal regulations, all at the risk of being penalised or taxed into ruin if you breach the regulations.

Simply getting property into your SMSF can be a challenge. Your SMSF deed must permit the proposed activities, after which you need to take into account the relevant property market risks along with the costs of complying with SMSF regulations. Then, if you are allowed to borrow, the potential lenders will need to understand and be comfortable with your proposed arrangements.

Your SMSF must be run for the sole purpose of providing superannuation benefits for its members, based on a rational investment strategy. For this reason, the following activities are not permitted:

- Lending money or provide financial assistance to a member or relative.

- Intentionally acquiring assets from related parties (though there are some exceptions, such as property that is used wholly or exclusively in a business and where the in-house asset test is satisfied).

- Borrowing money (except for Limited Recourse Borrowing Arrangements, which are used solely for the acquisition of a single asset, being a commercial or residential property).

- Charging benefits or assets.

- Undertaking transactions that are not at an arm's length. An arm's length transaction is one in which the parties are acting independently and have no relationship to each other. Therefore, transactions that are not at an arm's length are those where you're dealing with related parties.

One thing that *isn't* restricted is the ability of your SMSF to carry on a business. However, you cannot run a business that contravenes the requirement that a SMSF can only be operated to provide retirement benefits. As a simple example, this requirement would be breached if a SMSF fund member dipped into the fund to get cash to prop up his or her struggling business activities.

The benefits of using your SMSF for property development include:

- If you hold the property until retirement and you go into the pension phase, you will pay no tax on either the capital gain if you sell or the rent if you continue to hold your investment.

- Prior to retirement, the capital gains from selling your investment and any rent you earn from the investment is taxed at 15 per cent. There is an added bonus, from a capital gains point of view, if you have held the investment for more than 12 months, whereby the tax reduces further, down to as low as ten per cent for the capital gain.

- The ability to borrow to invest in direct property enables you to access high-growth assets without the need to pay for them upfront (remembering that if you are looking to develop the property, you will need to do so with clear funds in the SMSF).

- Investing in direct property in your SMSF gives you control of your investments and a real understanding of where your money is invested, as opposed to managed share schemes in traditional investment strategies.

- The long-term benefits of holding property with significant growth in value will supplement other investments within the SMSF. If borrowed funds are used to acquire these properties initially, it provides you with the opportunity to hold and develop those properties once the borrowing is cleared. That will accelerate the value growth in your SMSF far greater than cash or other traditional investments.

Getting it wrong

It's important to keep in mind that SMSFs are highly regulated and are under close scrutiny from the ATO, with significant consequences if you get it wrong,

The ATO has a range of penalties to encourage compliance, with the obligation on fund auditors to notify the ATO of any breaches:

- **Education direction:** The requirement to undertake a course of education designed to improve your competency and your ability to meet the regulatory obligations and reduce the risk of contravening the laws in the future.

- **Enforceable undertaking:** The requirement to commit in writing that you will stop the behaviour that led to the contravention. That you will rectify the contravention in an acceptable timeframe and to put in place strategies to prevent the contravention from reoccurring.

- **Rectification direction:** The requirement to undertake specific action to rectify the contravention within a specified time and provide evidence of the rectification.

- **Administrative penalties:** Trustees of the SMSF are personally liable to pay an administrative penalty for contravention of the superannuation laws. This can be a much as $10,800 per trustee. If you have four individual trustees, that totals $43,200. These penalties cannot be paid or reimbursed from the superannuation fund.

- **Disqualification of a trustee:** The ATO may disqualify an individual from acting as a trustee or a director of a corporate trustee if they contravene the superannuation laws.

For the more serious cases, a fund can be made non-complying, with the consequences including tax in the non-compliance year imposed at the top marginal tax rate on the market value of fund assets, minus contributions not counted as income. For example, if your SMSF has total assets of $2 million, you would be taxed at 49 per cent on 2017 rates, being $980,000. I think you'd agree – that's a fair incentive to get it right.

While this is clearly an outcome reserved for the most serious cases, it could be a very expensive mistake to assume that you will be able to talk your way out of any problems if the ATO is unhappy with your SMSF activities, particularly given the ATO warnings about audit activity.

Structuring within your SMSF

Assuming that all the regulatory requirements can be satisfied, it may be possible for your SMSF to be undertaking activities in a number of ways, including:

- As sole owner of the project, using SMSF funds

- By a limited recourse borrowing arrangement

- JV or as tenants in common

- By investing via unit trusts.

All of these options have their own pros and cons, and your particular circumstances and financial goals will need to be carefully considered when deciding which is right for you.

Sole owner

Simply put, this is where you use the cash funds within your SMSF to acquire and/or develop land. This option may be suitable where you have the required funds to complete the acquisition and/or development without the need to borrow.

It has the benefit of resulting in 100 per cent ownership of the developed property in the name of your SMSF. However, the constraints are that you may not be able to acquire and/or develop the size of project that will derive the greatest benefit.

Starting small and diversifying within your SMSF portfolio is a positive strategy.

Limited Recourse Borrowing Arrangement (LRBA)

Under an LRBA, your SMSF will have the potential to acquire land/property that might otherwise be out of your reach with the ability to borrow.

The restriction is that you will not be permitted to develop that land/property until such time as there is no borrowing attached to the asset. Therefore, this strategy is a longer-term option.

Keep in mind that, because your superannuation is meant for retirement, a long-term option can be a very successful strategy.

JV or tenants in common

In a JV arrangement, your SMSF will partner with other/s to acquire and/or develop property. Like the LRBA option, this will potentially provide the ability to access larger scale development opportunities with a capital injection from your JV partners.

Ensuring that all activities are conducted at an arm's length it could provide a successful result, particularly with the right JV partners involved in the development.

Dealing with a JV partner may present some issues, not unlike dealing with any business partner, and as such greater importance in this structure is placed on developing a clear plan and strategy for the development from the outset.

Unit trusts

Unit trusts, be they related or un-related trusts, are another option for investing your SMSF funds.

Related unit trusts

A related party is either a close family member, a partner in a partnership, and a company or a trust that is controlled or significantly influenced by a member of the SMSF.

A related unit trust is a trust where an SMSF member and/or his or her associates either hold more than 50 per cent equity, exercises significant influence in relation to the trust, or can appoint or remove the trustee.

In summary, a related trust is where there are related parties involved.

Legislation allows your SMSF to invest in a related unit trust provided that, at the time the interest is acquired, the unit trust does not have any:

- Interests in other entities

- Outstanding borrowings

- Charges over its assets

- Loans to other entities

- Leases with SMSF related parties (except in relation to properties used solely within a business)

- Assets acquired from related parties (unless they are business properties or the assets were acquired by the unit trust more than three years before the SMSF acquired the interest in the trust).

The investment cannot amount to more than five per cent of your SMSF's total assets. For example, if the SMSF has a total asset value of $1,000,000, they cannot invest more than $50,000 in a related trust.

Given the five per cent rule and the inability of the related unit trust to borrow, charge its assets or carry on a business, the SMSF may be limited in the context of property development activities. These restrictions do not apply to SMSF investments in unrelated entities.

Unrelated unit trust

An unrelated trust is one where there is no connection between the members of the SMSF and the trustees of the unit trust.

Investment in this type of entity is popular from a property development point of view when you want to share in the potential significant gains of property development without having to be involved with the development itself.

It has the added benefit of providing you access to much larger developments with greater returns than you would potentially be able to, given your balance within your own SMSF.

Subject to satisfying all the superannuation industry supervision (SIS) regulations and having a prudent investment strategy, your SMSF can invest in unrelated entities, including those that hold property, borrow money and carry out property development activities.

The threshold requirement is that the unit trust is unrelated to the SMSF for SIS purposes. This means that a member of the SMF cannot control the trust either by entitlement to 50 per cent or more of the income or capital of the trust, or have the power to appoint or remove the trustee.

An unrelated trust structure could possibly involve two unrelated SMSFs each with 50 per cent of the units, 50 per cent of the shares and 50 per cent of director voting power in the trustee company.

Assuming that the ATO (or a court) can be satisfied that you have an unrelated trust (and there are no other areas of SIS risk), and investing in the trust is prudent and fits within the SMSF investment strategy, then this is a way for the SMSF to have involvement in property development.

The commercial and legal aspects of an investment of this type also need to be carefully considered, including:

- The SMSF deed must permit the investment.

- Fifty per cent control is not effective commercial control.

- Unrelated investors may have different views about how things should work, and the terms of the arrangement should be carefully worked through and fully documented.

- Lenders may need to be convinced that the structure doesn't offend SIS rules.

There are no specific restrictions on the activities an unrelated trust can undertake, and there can be borrowings in an unrelated trust that undertakes property development activities.

Importantly, a unit trust in which one or more superannuation funds hold entitlements to more than twenty per cent of income and capital and which carries on a business (other than investment) is treated as a Public Trading Trust and taxed as a company, so that distributions are taxed as franked dividends.

Finally, if the ATO considers that income derived from unit trust holdings is not arm's length, the income in question can be taxed at the top marginal tax rate. This could occur where units are issued below market value, or other income is injected into the unit trust, and ends up in the hands of the SMSF unit holder.

SUMMARY

There are a range of potential structures you could use for your property development business, each of which comes with different benefits and risks. Choosing the right one can lead to tax concessions and higher profits, while the wrong one could result in higher costs and potential liability. The key is assessing your situation (including your existing business concerns) and intentions for the development in order to choose the right option for you.

APPENDIX C:
PROPERTY DEVELOPMENT AND GST

There are many Goods and Services Tax (GST) implications for property development businesses and, without a good working knowledge of these implications, you may find yourself in a tricky situation.

In this discussion, I'll outline the basics of how GST works, whether or not you need to register for GST, how business losses will affect your GST payments, how to avoid the GST pitfalls and when you should consider cancelling your GST.

An introduction to GST

Under the GST Act, an entity is liable to pay GST on 'taxable supplies' that it makes, and it is entitled to input tax credits for its 'creditable acquisitions'. In other words, you are entitled to pay GST on your income/revenue and you are also entitled to a refund of GST on your acquisitions/purchases.

For each tax period (normally three months or a quarter), the amount of GST you must pay for the revenue your business has generated is offset against the credits you are entitled to receive based on the business purchases you have made. The net amount is the amount that you must pay to the ATO (or which the ATO must pay to you) for that period.

In some cases, adjustments may be required from prior periods.

Simple enough?

Not quite.

GST only applies to certain types of revenue and certain types of purchases, rather than all of them. You need to know which is which in order to ensure that you clearly understand your GST liability.

Input taxed supplies are one exception, with the most common example being the lease of a residential property. In this case, no GST is payable on rental income earned. Similarly, no credits are available for any purchases that are related to earning that income (such as renovations).

Additionally, some purchases can be wholly creditable (meaning you can claim all of the GST charged), partly creditable (you can claim part of the GST charged) or not creditable (you cannot claim the GST). This depends on whether the entity has a 'creditable purpose', meaning whether, and to what extent, the purchase was made in order for you to run your business.

As you can see, there are many considerations when it comes to GST.

Do you need to register for GST?

If you are carrying on an enterprise you are entitled to register for GST. When your GST turnover exceeds the turnover threshold, you *must* register for GST.

An 'enterprise' includes activities done as part of an ongoing business and one-off activities that share the characteristics of a business dealing (such as running a one-off event for which you sell tickets). You can see from that definition, that the enterprise (or business) does not need to have a great level of sophistication or longevity. It simply needs to have a commercial or business characteristic of providing a product or service for a monetary or like reward.

However, an enterprise does not include activities done as a private recreational pursuit or hobby, or activities you might do without a reasonable expectation of profit or gain.

This means that private dealings among family members without an expectation of profit and dealings by hobbyists are likely to fall outside the scope of GST law.

When it comes to GST turnover, this is determined by calculating the total value of your sales excluding GST, input-taxed sales (sales where GST does not apply) and sales not connected to Australia.

There are two registration thresholds – the current turnover threshold and the projected turnover threshold. The current turnover threshold counts your GST turnover in the current month and the previous eleven months. The projected turnover threshold counts the turnover in the current month and the turnover likely to be achieved in the next eleven months. The threshold amount for both thresholds is $75,000 per annum.

It's also important to keep in mind two additional categories of supply that are not counted.

The first category is any income made, or likely to be made, by way of the transfer of ownership of a capital asset. Capital assets are structural assets – such as factories, shops or offices – through which a business is run. If you are registered for GST, you are liable for GST if you sell a capital asset in the course of your enterprise.

Capital assets are to be distinguished from revenue assets, such as trading stock. However, the character of an asset can change from capital to revenue and vice versa depending on how it is used. For property developers, properties built for sale and the land on which they are to be built are generally treated as revenue assets and rental properties, and the land on which they are to be built are generally treated as capital assets.

The second category is any income made, or that is likely to be made, as a consequence of ceasing to carry on an enterprise or substantially reducing the size or scale of an enterprise. For instance, if you purchase vacant land as a potential development site and decide not to proceed with any development activities, you would not be required to include the proceeds of the disposal of the land in your projected turnover.

So, the short answer to whether or not you need to register for GST is to look at your development activities and your GST turnover. If you are running an enterprise and your turnover it is over $75,000 per annum, you do need to register, whereas if it's under the threshold and/or you are not running an enterprise, you don't.

What happens if you change the use of your development?

What happens if you are a GST-registered property developer who builds apartments exclusively for sale, and later decides to rent them?

The typical situation is that you would start out by correctly claiming input tax credits on all acquisitions relating to the development, including architect's fees, legal fees and construction charges. However, when sales are slow or financial pressures arise, you then rent the apartments for income while still trying to actively sell them.

This is a change of use from a fully creditable purpose to a partly creditable application and will lead to a requirement to repay some of the GST credits claimed on the inputs into the development. The adjustment will be an increasing adjustment.

Contrary to popular belief, the increasing adjustment need not be made in the next activity statement due after an apartment is first leased. Nor is the GST repaid in a lump sum. The adjustment is made progressively at the end of an adjustment period.

An adjustment period for an acquisition or importation is a tax period that starts at least twelve months *after* the end of the tax period during which you started renting out the properties, and ends on 30 June in any year.

If you report on a monthly basis, rental income earned in April 2013 would not have its first adjustment period until 30 June 2014. If you report quarterly and receive rental income in April 2013, the first adjustment period for the acquisition would be June 2015. The reason for this is that the quarterly reporter's tax period ends on 30 June 2013 and the adjustment period must end on a 30 June that is at least twelve months *after* 30 June 2013. It can be seen, that 30 June 2014 does not fit this description as it falls *within* 12 months, not *after* 12 months.

How do business losses affect GST?

The ATO identifies a profit motive as one of the key indicators of an intention to carry on an enterprise. For this reason, the ATO places heavy emphasis on the achievement of profits.

A business that consistently operates at a loss and does not have a reasonable prospect of achieving profits in the short term is at risk of having its GST registration cancelled and its GST credit claims recovered.

If you're in this position as a developer, you may be required to defend yourself by objecting to the assessments issued and cancellation action taken by the ATO.

This would not be overly difficult where you have planned a development, as your project will likely be costed and the relevant research undertaken to determine that a potential profit is likely at completion and sale of the developed property. It is unlikely that you would proceed with any significant development without expert opinion regarding the build and the potential sales values. You would engage builders and real estate agents and any other relevant external party to quantify and qualify your development. The level of investment would warrant such activity.

Where the development is significant in size and therefore time, it may run over a number of financial years. If this is the case, the business may be reporting a loss based on the fixed overheads of running the business, not the variable costs directly related to the development. The reason for this is that the variable costs directly related to the development would be treated as trading stock and/or work-in-progress and therefore not have an impact on your profit or loss.

As explained in Appendix A, trading stock is added back at the end of the financial year if that land is not sold. Similarly, any development costs relating to an incomplete project will also be added back and therefore not impact on the profit or loss of the business, as the project is not yet complete and therefore not sold. At sale, all work-in-progress is taken up against the sale, as is the trading stock – that is, the cost of the original land.

The ATO and the courts will seek to determine the prospective profitability and/or the strong likelihood of it in any development as a positive indicator of the most important criteria for whether someone is carrying on a business (and by extension an enterprise), namely, the intention to make a profit.

It can be tricky, but always best to be informed irrespective of how the cards may fall.

What concessions are there for GST?

There are two key concessions for GST that apply to property developers – the margin scheme and how GST applies to going concerns (properties that deliver rental income).

Going concern

A sale of business where all that is necessary to operate the business is transferred to the purchaser is known as the supply of a 'going concern'. In simple terms, the business has the ability to continue to function, as was the case immediately prior to sale.

The revenue generated is GST-free if it is in exchange for money (or some other benefit), if the recipient is registered for GST (or required to be), and if the parties have agreed in writing that the business will continue to operate effectively.

There are two farm land concessions. The more common concession arises where:

a. There is a sale of land on which a farming business has been carried on for five years or more preceding the sale.

b. The purchaser intends that a farming business continues to be carried out on the land.

There is no defined time limit when it comes to the second criteria. However, there would be an adjustment if you tried to exit the GST system with the land or use it to make input taxed supplies.

A less commonly used concession is available where:

a. Potential residential land is subdivided from land on which a farming business has been carried on for at least five years.

b. The sale is made to an associate of the seller without consideration or for consideration below the GST-inclusive market value of the supply.

This concession allows potential residential land (land that it is permissible to use for residential purposes, but that does not contain any residential buildings) to be sold to a family member for development or for resale to a developer.

What does this all mean in real life situations?

If you intend to undertake a development in a business-like manner that constitutes an enterprise, you should consider becoming registered for GST as soon as the enterprise commences.

Consider the following example from the ATO of what it would consider activities organised in a business-like manner.

'Tony is a carpenter. After reading the Investors Club News, *he decides to purchase a property. He thoroughly researches the real estate market, attends investment seminars and records the information he has found.*

The property Tony purchases is in a good location but he pays a reduced price because it needs extensive renovation. Using his knowledge and contacts within the building industry, Tony quickly completes the renovations.

He then sells the property and makes a generous profit.

Using the proceeds from the sale of the first property, Tony purchases two more houses that require renovation.

Tony sets up an office in one of the rooms in his house. He has a computer and access to the internet so he can monitor the property market. Tony's objective is to identify properties that will increase in value over a short time once he has improved them. He leaves his job so he can spend more time on his research and renovations.

Tony's activities show all the factors that would be expected from a person carrying on a business. His property renovating operation demonstrates a profit-making intention; there is repetition and regularity to his activities. Tony's activities are organised in a business-like manner.

Therefore, Tony is regarded as being in the business of property renovation.'[2]

Identifying the commencement of your enterprise (in contrast to preparing to commence your enterprise) is a difficult task. The commencement of your enterprise usually coincides with the first significant expense incurred once your decision to proceed with a specific development has been made.

You are not required to be registered until sales are excess of the GST turnover threshold are made or are likely to be made. However, delaying registration in these circumstances is only going to inconvenience you and potentially enhance cash flow pressures. If you are likely to exceed the GST turnover threshold, you would be best advised to register from the beginning so you can claim any GST on your expenses, otherwise you could be faced with the scenario that the ATO would require you to be registered and therefore you would be out-of-pocket with GST payable on your sales, having not planned and managed your cash flow accordingly.

On the other hand, if you are undertaking a residential development and intend to hold the developed residential properties for rent, you should not apply to become registered. If you are already registered, you should consider applying for a cancellation or using a different entity to hold these properties.

With most property developments, the acquisitions and input tax credits typically precede the payment of GST arising from the sales. This timing

---

2   "Are you in the business of renovating properties?" Australian Taxation Office. February 17, 2016. Accessed March 04, 2017. https://www.ato.gov.au/General/Capital-gains-tax/In-detail/ Real-estate/Are-you-in-the-business-of-renovating-properties-/?page=2.

difference usually sparks an interest and hence response from the ATO. You are advised to ensure that your input tax credit claims are creditable acquisitions and supported by tax invoices before making the credit claims.

Margin scheme

The margin scheme is a way of working out the GST you must pay when selling a property that is a part of your business.

Where the margin scheme does not apply (in most cases), you would calculate the GST as one-eleventh of the sale price. Where the margin scheme does apply, you calculate the GST as one-eleventh of the 'margin'.

The margin is the difference between the sale price and the purchase price of the property. For property purchased prior to 1 July 2000, you have the choice to use the original purchase price or an approved valuation as of 1 July 2000.

It is important to note that the margin is not the profit you make on the property sale, as it does not take into account costs to develop the property or costs to subdivide the land.

If the property is sold as part of the business and is registered for GST, you may be able to use the margin scheme to work out how much GST you must pay. For example, if you purchased your property for $500,000 and sold it for $830,000 and the margin scheme applied, the total GST would be $30,000 (one-eleventh of the margin of $330,000), rather than $75,454 (which would be based on the sale price without the margin, or one-eleventh of $830,000).

Whether you can use the margin scheme depends on how and when you first purchased your property. You can use the margin scheme if you purchased the property before 1 July 2000 or if it is purchased after 1 July 2000 from someone who:

- Was not registered or required to be registered for GST

- Who sold you an existing residential premises

- Who sold the property to you as part of a GST-free going concern

- Who sold you the property using the margin scheme.

You cannot use the margin scheme if, when you first purchased the property, the sale was fully taxable and the margin scheme was not used. In this case, the amount of GST included in the price you paid is one-eleventh of the full purchase price.

The rules regarding the application of the margin scheme to a sale by you, as the developer, are very useful to understand. They provide mainly for situations in which your acquisition of the property to be developed makes the subsequent sale ineligible for the margin scheme.

The most common of these situations is where the entire interest in the property is acquired as fully taxable income on which GST is calculated without using the margin scheme (as detailed earlier).

Another common situation is where the entire interest in the property was acquired as a going concern from a vendor who had acquired the property as a fully taxable supply on which GST was calculated without using the margin scheme.

Where you acquire a property as a going concern from a vendor who was entitled to use the margin scheme (but didn't), you calculate the margin by deducting the vendor's purchase price (or the market value when the vendor purchased the property) from the sale price. For example, you purchased a property from a vendor as a going concern for $500,000. The vendor originally purchased the property for $400,000. You sell the property three years later for $600,000. You are able to calculate the margin on the vendor's original purchase price of $400,000. Therefore, your margin would be $200,000 and you would pay GST of one-eleventh of $200,000, being $18,182. If you do not apply the margin scheme, you would pay GST on the $600,000 sale price, being $54,545.

The best outcome for you is to purchase a property that is either an existing residence (on which no GST is payable) or a non-taxable supply (such as a commercial property sold by a vendor who is neither registered nor required to be). You then deduct the entire purchase price when calculating the taxable margin.

As a property developer, acquiring property as a going concern or as farm land is more attractive than acquiring it as a fully taxable supply, on which GST is worked out without applying the margin scheme. As long as you are eligible to use the margin scheme, you will save GST payable on the sale of the developed properties – generally one-eleventh of the acquisition value that can be used to calculate the taxable margin.

Can you avoid the GST pitfalls?

Many of the pitfalls that you could be faced with as the property developer can be avoided by asking some key what, who, how and why questions in the early stages.

Many of these pitfalls begin with the acquisition and in particular the contract of purchase. Things like:

- Is the property actually subject to GST?

- Is the vendor registered for GST? Should they be?

- Is the margin scheme applicable?

- Is it a sale of a going concern? Is that stated in the contract?

Not knowing the answers to these questions could have you claiming GST when you are not permitted and then having to repay that GST, possibly with interest and penalties. Alternatively, you may not have claimed the GST when in fact you possibly could.

What?

What is it that you are purchasing to develop? Is it vacant land, farm land, residential property, operating or non-operating commercial residential premises, leased or vacant commercial premises, or a mixed site (for instance, a downstairs shop and an upstairs residential apartment)?

You need to confirm that the vendor has adopted the correct and optimum GST treatment in the contract of sale. The simple approach of accepting that GST is to be added or included in the contract price (and can be recovered by the developer as an input tax credit) should be questioned and only accepted if no other GST treatments are available.

In a 2013 Supreme Court of Victoria case, two parties were in dispute over whether a property's contract price (around $900,000) included ten per cent GST.

The property was an existing residence and the sale that was not subject to GST, but the purchaser argued that the contract was GST-inclusive, and therefore the total price of the property should be reduced to $818,181. The vendor, on the other hand, argued that the contract was GST-exclusive, so the sale price should hold at $990,000.

The court found that the purchaser was required to complete the contract. With a better understanding of the GST issues the dispute could have been fully and simply resolved during the contract negotiations.

Who?

Who is the supplier of the development site? Is the vendor named in the contract of sale acting as a trustee of a trust, as a nominee or agent, or as a bare trustee?

If the contract provides for the sale to be plus GST, or a GST-free supply of a going concern, you should confirm that the supplier is in fact registered for GST.

Some unregistered vendors of commercial property are unaware of the exclusion for the sale of capital assets and register for GST so that they can charge, collect and remit the GST. This is incorrect on so many levels, as it adds to your duty liability and financial pressure, it sets you up for an early review by the ATO and it renders you ineligible to use the margin scheme upon resale.

A 2010 case in the Supreme Court of New South Wales heard two parties dispute the contract price of a residential apartment above a fruit shop that had been sold at auction. The vendor insisted that it was plus GST and the purchaser insisted that it was GST inclusive.

The vendor proved to the satisfaction of the judge that the auction had been conducted on the basis that a further ten per cent would be added for GST.

When a ruling was sought from the ATO as to the amount of GST required to be paid (the fruit shop being commercial premises and the apartment being residential), the Commissioner ruled that the sale was not a taxable supply to any extent because the vendor was neither GST-registered nor required to be.

The second 'who' to consider is who is the developer entity?

Where a property is being acquired and there is flexibility for deciding which entity is going to make the acquisition, you should give careful consideration to the entity that is going to undertake the development. Individuals and partnerships of individuals carry inherent risks as do partnerships of companies or trusts. (Refer to the Appendix B: Structuring your property development, for more information.)

The decision should be made carefully and with regard to issues of asset protection, income tax and GST.

How?

How is GST accounted for in the contract of sale? Is it expressly stated? Is there a clause defining the exact treatment of GST? Has this been correctly stated?

The GST clause in a typical contract of sale for real estate will offer several GST outcomes to choose from, including plus GST, inclusive of GST, margin scheme, supply of a going concern and farm land.

Rented residential premises should never be acquired as a going concern as this may render you liable to a non-creditable increasing adjustment, applicable where going concerns are acquired with a view to making input taxed supplies.

The failure to adopt the most appropriate GST treatment in the contract may also deny you access to the margin scheme upon resale and embroil you in a costly, time consuming and avoidable contractual dispute.

In 2013 the Supreme Court of Victoria handed down its decision in a case where the parties were in dispute as to whether the contract price was inclusive of or plus GST. (The case had been back and forth to that court since 2008!)

The purchaser made an offer of $2,250,000 for the property, which the vendor accepted. However, the contract of sale contained a GST clause and a dispute later arose between the parties as to whether the GST clause required the purchaser to pay an additional $225,000 to the vendor on account of GST.

The judge decided that the GST clause was obscure and meaningless and did not clearly state whether the parties intended the price to be inclusive or exclusive of GST. The court declared the clause was void for uncertainty and severable from the contract.

Why?

Why are you acquiring the property? If the development involves the construction of residential premises, are they for sale or for rent? These questions are directly relevant to your decision to register for GST and to your entitlement to recover in full, partially or not at all, the cost of any GST imposed on the construction inputs.

Sometimes you will be undecided about your plans to sell or rent. This complicates the decision-making about registration and the claiming of input tax credits. These issues should be identified and confronted by you sooner rather than later. To do otherwise is to risk a GST compliance nightmare.

In Appendix A, I discussed the implications of a change of purpose for your development. This is particularly important when it comes to GST.

You need to have a clear intention as that will determine whether or not you are required to register for GST and/or can claim GST on acquisitions and whether there will be GST on sales. However, intentions can change.

You may have intended to develop your land with three townhouses and sell all three. In so doing, you claim back GST on those acquisitions, say $120,000. At the completion of the development, the market conditions are such that you believe you would be best to hold and rent with a view to selling some time in the future. At that point, the $100,000 of GST you have already claimed back from the ATO will need to be repaid. This will likely have significant cash flow implications, as you would have likely used those funds to assist with the costs of development and, as such, do not have access to the funds anymore. In addition, you have likely borrowed for the development and, depending on how that debt was structured, the banks may also be seeking repayment in some form.

I think you can now clearly see the importance of intention and, where possible, planning accordingly.

You must document your intentions at the time of acquisition and monitor changes of use (if any) for the change of use adjustments described above.

Documentation

So many legal cases are decided against taxpayers because they are unable to prove that the taxation decision should have been made differently. Unfortunately, the onus is on *you*.

Evidence in the form of emails, text messages, letters and file notes is vital to support your claims of intended use in any dispute with the ATO. The support of third parties, such as agents and financiers, is also extremely useful.

When should you consider cancelling your GST registration?

Just as not being registered for GST (or required to be registered) can be an effective defence against an accusation that you have made a taxable income, legitimately cancelling your registration before the income is made can prevent the income from being taxable.

The cancellation process involves applying for the cancellation with the ATO. You are required to have done one of two things before you apply to cancel your GST registration:

1. Ceased trading or now trading under the GST turnover threshold.

2. Sold the business to another party.

If you leave the GST system, you are required to make an increasing adjustment in your final return.

If you apply for cancellation more than twelve months after becoming registered and the ATO is satisfied that you are not required to be registered, the ATO must cancel your registration.

Note that you are not required to have ceased operations. However, the ATO must be satisfied that your annual turnover is below the current and projected registration thresholds. Hence, you can cancel even if you are continuing to carry on an enterprise – as long as your turnover does not require you to be registered.

If you have ceased operations, the ATO can cancel your registration upon becoming satisfied that you are not carrying on an enterprise and that registration is not likely to be required for at least twelve months.

The ATO may also cancel your registration if you have been registered for less than twelve months and they are satisfied that you are not required to be registered.

This is important because there will be times when your best outcome is to purchase or sell property as a non-taxable source of revenue. One scenario would be if your current and projected GST turnover is below the threshold and you wish to sell a capital asset without paying GST.

In making this decision you will need to consider whether your current and projected GST turnover are below the threshold and the size of any increasing adjustment that may be required to make upon cancellation.

When the ATO cancels a GST registration, it will notify you of the date of effect of the cancellation and alert you to the possibility of an increasing adjustment.

SUMMARY

As a property developer, it's essential to be aware of the complexities of dealing in real property and the GST implications of this. In simple terms, you are required to pay GST on your income/revenue once your GST turnover crosses the $75,000 threshold. You are also entitled to a refund on the GST you have paid for relevant purchases.

Keep in mind that the reality is more complex than that, particularly when it comes to changing your development intentions, making the most of concessions and avoiding the pitfalls, so this is an area where professional advice is essential.

APPENDIX D:
THE SMALL BUSINESS RESTRUCTURE ROLLOVER

The ATO's Small Business Restructure Rollover gives you flexibility, as an owner of a small business entity, to restructure your businesses and the way your business assets are held while disregarding tax gains and losses that would otherwise arise.

There is a range of small business rollovers already available where you – as an individual, trustee or partner – transfer assets to, or creates assets in, a company while incorporating your business. These rollovers include:

- The transfer of assets or a business from an individual, trustee or partner to a wholly owned company (Division 122 rollovers).

- The transfer of assets or a business from a trust to a company (Subdivision 124-N rollover).

- Division 615 rollovers where an interest holder exchanges shares in a company or units in a unit trust for shares in another company as part of a restructure.

These rollovers deal with the transfer of assets to a company or deal with shares or interests in companies. However, they are limited as they only apply in the following cases:

- When assets are transferred into companies (not where assets are transferred out of companies or between entities that are not companies).

- When shares or interests in companies and trusts are exchanged for shares in companies.

The Small Business Restructure Rollover, on the other hand, is not restricted to the transfer of assets to companies. While this rollover can also be used where business assets are transferred to a company, it also allows for the transfer of assets from:

a. Individual(s) to trusts or companies

b. Partnership assets by partners to trusts or companies

c. Company assets to trusts

d. Company assets to individuals and partnerships

e. Trust assets to beneficiaries of trusts

f. Transfer of assets from one trust to another.

Uses for the new rollover

The new rollover has a range of uses for property developers, with the two most pertinent being trust cloning and demerger relief.

Trust cloning

The Small Business Restructure Rollover is particularly useful for trust entities, given that trusts are a very common business or investment structure. The new rollover will allow the transfer of assets from one trust to another trust using trust cloning techniques without adverse income tax consequences.

For example, a trust holding both real property and active business assets may, for asset protection purposes, transfer the business assets to another trust that has the same beneficiaries as the transferor trust. Such transfers are now permitted and will increase asset protection of your real property from your business.

Prior to the introduction of the rollover, trust cloning was still a viable option for trustees, however, CGT provisions applied to the transfer and unless the trustees could access the CGT concessions, such as the small business CGT concessions, then it would be liable for the CGT on transfer.

This CGT liability has now effectively been removed so the transfer can take place without triggering a CGT liability.

The rollover does not require the cloned trust to be identical to the original trust. The only requirement is that there is 'no practical change' in which individuals economically benefit for the assets of the trust, both before and after the rollover.

Demerger relief

A demerger involves restructuring a corporate or fixed trust group by split-ting its operations into two or more entities. Under a demerger, the owners of the head entity of the group (either shareholders or unit holders) acquire a direct interest (shares or units) in an entity that was formerly part of the group (the demerged entity).

The Small Business Restructure Rollover will effectively provide a shortcut for this process. Using the rollover, your assets may be transferred from one company to another company without suffering adverse tax consequences.

Opportunities may also arise for multi-stage restructuring.

For example, a husband and wife partnership may use the existing Division 122 Rollover to transfer partnership assets to a company in exchange for shares in that company. As a second step, using the Small Business Restructure Rollover, the shares in the company may be transferred to the corporate trustee of a discretionary family trust.

The two-step process would result in partnership business assets being held by a company with a corporate trustee of a family trust as the shareholder. This is a very common business structure used where cash has to be retained to expand the business.

The rollover opens up a number of planning opportunities, particularly with asset protection and business structuring.

Consequences of rollover

Income tax neutral

The Small Business Restructure Rollover is intended to be tax neutral to the extent that there should be no income tax consequences arising from the transfer of the assets.

Cost of assets transferred

In order to maintain tax neutrality, the transferor is deemed to have transferred assets at their rollover cost. The rollover cost is the transferor's cost for income tax purposes so that the transfer of the assets will not give rise in a gain or loss to the transferor. The transferee will be deemed to have acquired the assets at the transferor's cost just before the transfer.

The rollover cost is defined as the original cost for CGT assets, or written-down value for depreciating assets.

Pre-CGT assets

Pre-CGT assets, or assets that were acquired before 28 September 1985, retain their pre-CGT status when transferred under rollover.

CGT discount

An asset disposed of within twelve months of the transfer under the roll-over will not be eligible for the 50 per cent general CGT discount. The reason for this is that the rollover is targeted at genuine restructures of an ongoing business and is not intended to cover restructures to facilitate the sale of a business or asset shortly after the restructure.

This is very important to understand because if you want to proceed with the rollover so you can receive a benefit for accessing the 50 per cent CGT discount, then you should think again.

Membership interests as consideration for transfer of assets

The transfer of assets under the rollover may be to an entity that is able to issue membership interests, such as a company or a unit trust. Where part or all of the consideration for the transfer is the issue of membership interests, the first element of the membership interests' cost base or reduced cost base, as defined in Section 328-465 of the ITAA 1997, is the sum of:

- The rollover costs of the CGT assets (excluding pre-CGT assets) transferred, plus

- The adjustable value of depreciating assets transferred

Less

- Any liabilities assumed or taken on by the transferee

Divided by

- The number of membership interests.

Consider the following example from the Explanatory Memorandum of the new tax law bill.

> *'Edamame Pty Ltd transfers three assets that it owns to the Soy Trust in circumstances that qualify for rollover:*
>
> - *A CGT asset having a cost base of $100,000*
>
> - *A second CGT asset having a cost base of $1 million, and*
>
> - *A depreciating asset having an adjustable value of $400,000.*
>
> *The Multi-Level Trust issues ten units to Development Pty Ltd in exchange for the transfer.*
>
> *The cost base and reduced cost base of each unit is $150,000 [($100,000 + $1 million + $ 400,000)/10].'*[3]

Where the consideration for the transfer of assets is only partly made up of the issue of membership interests, the first element of the cost base/ reduced cost base of the membership interests is reduced accordingly.

In the above example, if Edamame Pty Ltd had a liability of $300,000 attached to the second CGT asset and the Soy Trust assumed that liability as well as paying Edamame Pty Ltd an amount of $500,000 under the transaction; the cost base and reduced cost base of each unit is: $70,000 [($100,000 + $1 million + $ 400,000 – $300,000 – $500,000)/10].

---

3   "SMALL BUSINESS RESTRUCTURE ROLL-OVER) BILL 2016 Explanatory Memorandum." Tax Laws Amendment. Accessed March 04, 2017. http://www.austlii.edu.au/au/legis/cth/bill_em/ tlabrrb2016622/memo_0.html.

The loss denial rule

The new rollover allows flexibility in the consideration (be that money or ownership in other interests) to be given for the transfer of assets. There is no requirement to transfer the assets at market value. In fact, it allows the consideration to be zero.

The transferor and transferee may agree to transfer the asset at its cost or some other amount other than the market value. Transfers of assets at other than market value will either increase or decrease the market value of any interests in the transfer or company or trust and in the company or trust issuing membership interests.

The Small Business Restructure Rollover includes the loss integrity rule to ensure that a capital loss on any direct or indirect membership interest in the transferor or transferee made, subsequent to the rollover, will be disregarded unless you can demonstrate that the loss is reasonably attributable to something other than the rollover.

In other words, you cannot transfer the assets to artificially create a loss in order to obtain a tax benefit.

The example from the Explanatory Memorandum of the new tax law bill is listed below:

'The Dance Partnership transfers an asset having an acquisition cost of $400,000 and market value of $500,000 to Studio Pty Ltd, and the Small Business Restructure Rollover applies to the transfer. Immediately prior to the transfer, Studio Pty Ltd had existing assets of $700,000 and eighteen ordinary shares on issue.

Studio Pty Ltd issues one share each to Riley and Michelle, the partners in the Dance Partnership, as consideration for the transfer.

For both Riley and Michelle, the cost base and reduced cost base for *their new share will be $200,000, and the post issue market value of that share will be $60,000.*

To claim a capital loss on subsequent disposal, Riley and Michelle would need to establish that the loss is attributable to something other than the rollover transaction which includes, relevantly, the issue of the shares and allocation of a $200,000 reduced cost base for those shares.

As the difference of $140,000 between the market value and the cost base of each share is attributable to the rollover transaction, Riley and Michelle will be unable to claim a loss to that extent on any subsequent disposal of the shares."[4]

Interaction with Small Business CGT Concessions

152-E – rollover relief

Where a transferor applies the rollover to transfer an asset that is a replacement asset (for instance, selling a business asset owned by one entity to buy shares owned by another entity), the transferee under the rollover is taken to have made the choice for the replacement asset, and CGT events may apply to the transferee. Effectively this means that those CGT events will not apply just because of the rollover, but may apply depending on how the asset is used or when it is disposed of by the transferee under the rollover.

152-B: 15-year exemption

For the purposes of the 15-year exemption, the transferee under a rollover will be taken to have acquired the asset subject to the rollover when the

---

4   "SMALL BUSINESS RESTRUCTURE ROLL-OVER) BILL 2016 Explanatory Memorandum." Tax Laws Amendment. Accessed March 04, 2017. http://www.austlii.edu.au/au/legis/cth/bill_em/tlabrrb2016622/memo_0.html.

transferor under the rollover acquired it. Effectively this means that the rollover will not break the ownership period for the purposes of claiming the 15-year exemption.

Case study

Bob and Lynne partnered to start a husband and wife plumbing business ten years ago, specialising in plumbing for large medical facilities such as hospitals and medical centres. Over the past ten years, the business has grown substantially and employs five plumbers. Five years ago, Bob and Lynne purchased a factory/warehouse from which the business is run.

Their current balance sheet discloses the following:

	Cost	Market value
Factory warehouse	$500,000	$1,000,000
Plant & Equipment	$300,000	$80,000
Stock	$150,000	$150,000
Goodwill	$0	$800,000
Less		
Factory/Warehouse loan	$400,000	$400,000

Bob and Lynne would like to restructure so that:

- They can protect their personal assets from business risk.

- Quarantine the factory warehouse from the risks of the plumbing business.

- Retain as much of the profit for future growth of the business.

- Reduce their tax liability.

Possible options include:

Transfer the factory/warehouse to a newly established discretionary trust with a family trust election, nominating Bob as the test individual. The net value of the factory/warehouse could be gifted to the trust, giving rise to an increase in trust capital (if the loan on the factory/warehouse has been paid out, the full value could be gifted); or for consideration with a loan payable by the discretionary trust to Bob and Lynne for the net value of the factory/warehouse. The discretionary trust could borrow funds to repay the factory/warehouse loan. The cost base of the factory/warehouse to the discretionary trust for CGT purposes will be $500,000. Duty will be payable on the transfer, but the rollover will mean that there will not be a CGT liability.

The transfer of the stock and Plant & Equipment to a trust or company entity will not give rise to adverse tax consequences because of the rollover relief provisions.

The transfer of stock will be at cost and any stock on hand at the beginning of the year will be transferred at the value used at the beginning of the year.

The Goodwill, Plant & Equipment and stock could be transferred to:

- A second discretionary trust with a family trust election nominating Bob as the test individual. This quarantines the Factory/Warehouse from the risks of the plumbing business. The cost base of the Goodwill will be zero for the second discretionary trust, or

- A company under a Division 122 rollover. Provided the shares in the company are active assets, the shares could be transferred to a discretionary trust that has made a family trust election with Bob or Lynne as the test individual.

In both cases, the cost base of the Goodwill will be zero and the Plant & Equipment will have a tax value of $80,000, being the adjustable or written-down value (cost less depreciation).

Bob and Lynne could choose to not apply the rollover, trigger a capital gain and apply the Division 152 small business CGT concession and get an uplift in the Goodwill cost base. This might be a useful strategy where the turnover and value of the business in increasing.

SUMMARY

The rollover provides a great deal of flexibility for your small business entities to move to more effective structures for taxation and asset protection purposes. However, my experience with the small business CGT concessions leads me to believe that the ATO will carefully scrutinise restructures to ensure they constitute genuine restructures, so it's best to get professional advice before restructuring.

ACKNOWLEDGEMENTS

To my beautiful children, Sarah, Samantha and Chris – thank you for giving me the extra passion for life that drives me to be the best I can be. Without you, this book would not have been written.

To my partner, Tanya – thank you for your love and understanding, particularly through the challenging period of writing this book.

To the inspirational Glen Carlson and his incredible team at Dent/ KPI – thank you for providing entrepreneurs the brilliant framework through which we can become Key People of Influence.

To the master author, Andrew Griffiths – thank you for your wisdom and encouragement to get pen to paper and share my knowledge with the world.

To Jacqui Pretty and the amazing team at Grammar Factory – thank you for providing my book with the cut and polish it needed to be able to proudly sit on bookshelves today.

To my business partner and life-long friend, David Azzopardi – thank you for your unwavering support and friendship. I love living the dream with you.

To all my family and friends – thank you for allowing me to be a part of your lives. Without you, life would not be as complete.

I cannot thank each and every one of you enough.

ABOUT THE AUTHOR

Tony Dimitriadis is a Certified Practising Accountant (CPA) and has success-fully run his tax and accounting firm, AD Partners, for over 15 years. In May 2014, he established his financial planning company, AD Wealth. He has also published a range of articles offering simple and practical tax and business advice online at www.adpartners.com.au.

Tony's extensive qualifications and experience in the financial and busi-ness sector have enabled him to help hundreds of businesses to greatly improve their financial position and establish future planning initiatives to create long-term wealth. Tony has saved a number of business owners from near bankruptcy, and completely turned their financial position around.

Tony is very passionate about his business and his clients and he fights to get them the best result, in all aspects of their businesses.

While Tony's clients hail from a variety of industries, the building and property development industry is one that has been pivotal to his own development and success as well as to the success of his clients.

Tony is best known for offering his clients a complete financial solution and helping them achieve their financial goals sooner and with significantly less stress and frustration along the journey.

After working with Tony, his clients feel extremely assured and positive about the future. They are taking back control of their business, delivering remarkable value and creating amazing opportunities to truly benefit their business and, ultimately, their lifestyle.

Tony's vision is that every business owner achieves financial freedom – the ability to have the money they desire and the time to use it any way they choose.

ABOUT AD PARTNERS

Do you want to start a highly profitable and successful building and property development business that empowers you to live the lifestyle you want?

If so, AD Partners can help.

AD Partners is an accounting firm that specialises in working with business owners in building and property development. Over the past 15 years they have worked with over 1,000 business owners and have helped then achieve remarkable results.

AD Partners has developed a proven Five S method:

1. **Strategy:** AD Partners will start by helping you create a strategic plan by assessing where you are now, deciding where you want to go and charting the most efficient course between the two.

2. **Structure:** Structure is an essential piece of achieving your strategic goals, so in this step AD Partners will help ensure you have the right structure for you and your business.

3. **Statutory:** Are you aware (and on top of) all of the obligations you have to the Australian Taxation Office (ATO), Australian Securities and Investment Commission (ASIC), State Revenue Office (SRO), Land Titles Office, WorkCover Authority, your superannuation provider and your bank? In this step, AD Partners will ensure you understand the main obligations you need to be aware of as an ambitious business owner.

4. **Systems:** In this step, AD Partners will help you put in place the main money management systems your business will need to stay on top of your obligations, while moving towards your strategic goals.

5. **Support:** As an ambitious business owner, you probably try to do it all yourself. The problem is that this isn't sustainable. This is why support is essential. In this step, AD Partners will be the right support team to help you implement the first four steps of the framework, while pushing your business on to bigger and better things.

If you found this book insightful and helpful and you're ready to get started, go to www.adpartners.com.au/financialhealthcheck for your free financial health check or contact AD Partners directly via telephone on +61 3 9349 3499 for your obligation-free thirty-minute consultation.

No need to wait any longer – contact AD Partners now – they're there for you.